BREAKAWAY

BREAK AWAY

The PWHL and the Women Who Changed the Game

KARISSA DONKIN

Edited by Jill Ainsley.
Cover and page design by Julie Scriver.
Cover image: PWHL Enterprises US LP.
Printed in Canada by Marquis.
10 9 8 7 6 5 4 3 2

Goose Lane Editions acknowledges the generous support of the Government of Canada, the Canada Council for the Arts, and the Government of New Brunswick.

Library and Archives Canada Cataloguing in Publication

Title: Breakaway : the PWHL and the women who changed the game / Karissa Donkin.
Names: Donkin, Karissa, author.
Identifiers: Canadiana (print) 20250185547 | Canadiana (ebook) 20250185563 | ISBN 9781773104362 (softcover) | ISBN 9781773104379 (EPUB)
Subjects: LCSH: Professional Women's Hockey League. | LCSH: Hockey for women—Canada. | LCSH: Hockey for women—United States.
Classification: LCC GV847.8.P76 D66 2025 | DDC 796.962/640820971—dc23

Goose Lane Editions is located on the unceded territory of the Wəlastəkwiyik whose ancestors along with the Mi'kmaq and Peskotomuhkati Nations signed Peace and Friendship Treaties with the British Crown in the 1700s.

Goose Lane Editions
500 Beaverbrook Court, Suite 330
Fredericton, New Brunswick
CANADA E3B 5X4
gooselane.com

For Papa Jack Donkin, who would have loved to read this with a cup of tea and a Leafs game on. Thank you for introducing me to this beautiful game.

CONTENTS

TIMELINE 9

PROLOGUE 13

1. NOWHERE TO PLAY 19

2. THE DREAM GAP 33

3. FOR THE GAME 45

4. THE VERDUN AUDITORIUM 57

5. A LEAGUE IS BORN 77

6. FROM THE GROUND UP 93

7. DRAFT DAY 103

8. MADAME SAUVAGEAU'S VISION 117

9. DROPPING THE PUCK 133

10. THE PAST, PRESENT, AND FUTURE 141

11. DANCING ON THE ICE 157

12. BATTLE ON BAY STREET 167

13. A PERSON FIRST, A HOCKEY PLAYER SECOND 181

14. SHE'S GAY, MARCUS 193

15. THE DUEL AT THE TOP 201

16. CHASING THE WALTER CUP 213

17. CROWNING A CHAMPION 227

EPILOGUE: VICTOIRE DE MONTRÉAL 235

ACKNOWLEDGEMENTS 243

TIMELINE

March 1990: The first Women's World Championship is held in Ottawa. Canada defeats the United States 5–2 for the gold.

February 1998: Women's hockey is part of the Olympic programme for the first time. The Americans defeat Canada 3–1 in Nagano, Japan, to win Olympic gold.

Fall 1998: The National Women's Hockey League (NWHL) replaces the Central Ontario Women's Hockey League (COWHL). In the first season, the league includes teams in Ontario and Quebec.

May 2007: The NWHL suspends operations. That summer, a group of players lead the creation of the Canadian Women's Hockey League (CWHL), which begins play in the fall of 2007.

October 2015: The four-team National Women's Hockey League (later rebranded as the Premier Hockey Federation) begins play in the United States. The league is separate from the Canadian league with the same name that folded in 2007.

March 2017: The players on the American women's national team announce they will withhold their labour at the Women's World

Championship in Michigan if they can't come to an agreement with USA Hockey on fair wages and equal support for training, accommodations, grassroots funding, and other issues. The governing body and the team reach a deal before the tournament begins. The Americans defeat the Canadians 3–2 in overtime to win gold in April 2017.

March 2019: The CWHL announces it will shut down on May 1, 2019.

May 2019: More than two hundred players vow to not play in any professional hockey league until their labour is compensated and they can play in professional conditions. Their goal is to create a "long-term viable professional league." The group becomes the Professional Women's Hockey Players Association (PWHPA).

September 2019: The PWHPA holds the first event on the Dream Gap Tour, a barnstorming tour across North America.

March 2020: The COVID-19 pandemic shuts down professional sports, halting the Dream Gap Tour and cancelling the Women's World Championship scheduled for April 2020.

April 2020: The NWHL announces plans to expand to Canada with a team in Toronto. The team is later named the Toronto Six.

September 2021: The NWHL is rebranded as the Premier Hockey Federation (PHF).

June 2023: An investor group led by Mark and Kimbra Walter buys the PHF, shuts the league down, and creates a new league called the Professional Women's Hockey League (PWHL). The league later announces it will have teams in Ottawa, Montréal, Toronto, the New York area, Minnesota, and Boston. The league is governed by a four-person advisory board that includes Billie Jean King, Ilana Kloss, Stan Kasten, and Royce Cohen.

July 2023: Players ratify the first collective bargaining agreement between the league and the PWHL Players Association.

September 2023: The PWHL holds its first draft. Forward Taylor Heise is the first overall pick, selected by Minnesota.

January 1, 2024: The first PWHL game takes place on New Year's Day inside Toronto's Mattamy Athletic Centre. New York defeats Toronto 4–0.

PROLOGUE

April 20, 2024
Montréal, Quebec

You could feel the excitement pulsing through the arena even before the Montréal players took the ice.

With a capacity of more than twenty-one thousand, the Bell Centre is the largest hockey arena in North America, and it's typically home to the NHL's Montréal Canadiens. But this day was all about PWHL Montréal, the team that had been the hottest ticket in town since the Professional Women's Hockey League launched in January.

It was Montréal against Toronto on a Saturday afternoon, and even though these two teams had existed for only four and a half months, the rivalry already felt deep. Montréal had yet to beat Toronto in four games head-to-head, and this was the last regular-season meeting between them. On this day, their audience was the largest crowd to ever watch a women's hockey game in person, breaking a record set just two months earlier when these two teams faced off inside Toronto's Scotiabank Arena. Beyond attendance records, playoff positions in the six-team league were at stake.

The league was so new that neither team had a logo or even a name yet, things that got put aside in the rush to get players on the ice as fast as possible in January. But none of these fans seemed to care. Tickets to this game sold out in twenty minutes. The crowd was full of maroon-and-cream jerseys that simply read *Montréal*, an ode to their team and city. Those jerseys had been sold out online for months, and lines to get one at a rink could be long. The arena glowed maroon mixed with tiny purple lights, thanks to the light-up wristbands handed out to every fan. The DJ blasted a remix of Celine Dion's "The Power of Love," the team's skate-out song throughout the inaugural season. When a shot of the players in the tunnel appeared on the jumbotron, with some of them vibing to Celine, the crowd roared.

First out of the tunnel was Ann-Renée Desbiens, the goaltender from Clermont, a small Quebec city that the Malbaie River runs through. She grew up dreaming of playing in big games. And to be clear, big games weren't new to her. She'd thrived in plenty of those as the starting goaltender for Team Canada, the team she'd backstopped to three world championships by that point and an Olympic gold medal. But this was a different stage. It was home. Desbiens was one of Montréal's first three signings when general manager Danièle Sauvageau started building this team brick by brick, and she was, and is, PWHL Montréal's backbone.

Farther behind, forward Catherine Dubois grinned from ear to ear as she skated out onto the Bell Centre ice. A few months ago, she was spending her days hauling heavy cement bricks on construction sites two-and-a-half hours away in Quebec City, where she worked in the family masonry business. At the time, Dubois was convinced her hockey career was over, and it wasn't the first time she'd had that feeling. Who could have imagined she would be here?

Last out was defender Erin Ambrose, whose eyes wandered through the stands as she moved forward, taken aback by the sight of twenty-one thousand white towels waving. It felt surreal to her. Unlike Desbiens and Dubois, Ambrose grew up cheering for the Toronto Maple Leafs. But Montréal had been her sanctuary in 2018 after getting cut from the Canadian Olympic team. Ambrose came to this city to run away from that disappointment and shame, but it became a place where she found joy playing hockey again. It had felt like a full-circle moment when Sauvageau picked her in the first round of the draft the previous September.

The players skated laps around their half of the ice before huddling around Desbiens in the net, a routine they did before every game. Across from Desbiens inside the huddle, in the middle of it all, was number 29: the captain, Marie-Philip Poulin. If Desbiens is the backbone of this team, Poulin is its heartbeat. When Montréal was announced as one of the first six PWHL teams, there was no question who would be the captain. It had to be Poulin. Nicknamed Captain Clutch for her ability to score big goals for Canada in the most important moments on the international stage, she's even more than that here in Montréal. She's the face of women's hockey. She's the name on half the signs in the stands, the player who always takes an extra second to speak to a wide-eyed child, who always remembers a girl who attended her annual summer hockey camp. She's the captain always eager to deflect attention to her teammates. That's never changed, no matter how many big goals she's scored.

The players skated to the blue line as the public address announcer began introducing the Toronto roster. The crowd cheered for the opposition, and it was so loud that players on the ice struggled to hear their names called. Standing on the blue line, Poulin couldn't imagine how loud the crowd would get for them if this was how loud they cheered for Toronto. The volume started to go up when Montréal players began hearing their names. Number 9, defender Kati Tabin. Number 23, defender Erin Ambrose. Number 43, forward Kristin O'Neill. Number 7, forward Laura Stacey. The cheering hit a crescendo when the announcer got to the captain.

"Number twenty-nine," he said. The crowd nearly drowned him out before he could say her name. "Marie-Philip Pouuuuuuuulin!"

Poulin, with a smile on her face, took a deep breath as she looked up at the crowd. She smiled and seemed to let the emotion fully hit her. It was an outpouring of love for the captain, for all the gold medals, for every autograph she'd ever stopped to sign, and for everything she means to Quebec. When the cheers continued for a solid twenty seconds, Poulin saluted the crowd with her stick and applauded them. *Is this for real?* Poulin asked herself as she stood on the blue line. Never a fan of the spotlight, she felt the moment lingered on her for a bit too long.

You could say Poulin had dreamed of that day her entire life, but that wouldn't be entirely true. The young girl who grew up playing with boys in Beauceville, a small city between Quebec City and Maine, never dreamed a women's hockey game could sell out the Bell Centre. She didn't think it was possible when, at sixteen, she came to this arena to watch her first Montréal Canadiens game, around the same time she moved to the city so she could follow her hockey dreams. She still didn't think it was possible a decade later in 2017, when she played a Canadian Women's Hockey League (CWHL) game here with Les Canadiennes. Fewer than six thousand people had shown up. She had looked up at the empty seats and let herself wish they'd be full someday. That league folded in 2019 and for a while, a scene like this seemed very far away.

Farther down the blue line, Ambrose managed to hold it together during Poulin's ovation. Poulin is her captain, but she's also one of her best friends. If you ask Ambrose, the hardest part about not playing in a league for four seasons wasn't just that she missed four years of the prime of her own career, finding herself without a place to play just after being crowned the CWHL's Defender of the Year with Les

Canadiennes. It was that the world missed four years of watching *Poulin* play in a league, four years we'll never get back. There will never be another player like Poulin, someone who blends her talent on the ice with her dogged work ethic and her unmatched ability to connect with her teammates. The creation of this league meant people could see Poulin play on a regular Tuesday night and not just when she put on a Team Canada jersey. Having the world see Poulin more often is something Ambrose thinks could grow the game to a whole new level.

On the Montréal bench, head coach Kori Cheverie held back tears, knowing the TV cameras would probably catch her crying. When she was growing up in Nova Scotia, Cheverie would get her mom to wake her up at five a.m. to catch replays of games from the old National Women's Hockey League, which operated from the 1998–99 season until 2007. She knew back then that she wanted to play professionally. She went on to play in the CWHL, winning a championship with the Toronto Furies in 2014. But the game at the Bell Centre was something entirely different than what she'd experienced in her playing career.

On the opposing bench, Toronto defender Lauriane Rougeau fought back tears, too. Poulin had lived with Rougeau's family when she moved to Montréal as a teenager. Rougeau had watched Poulin thrive at every level and watched her become the person she was today. They played together on Les Canadiennes, won an Olympic gold medal together a decade ago, and on this day, found themselves sharing this moment together on opposite sides of the rink, in what would be Rougeau's final season playing hockey.

High above in the press box was Isabelle Leclaire, working as an analyst with French sports network RDS. Leclaire had coached a shy, fifteen-year-old Poulin with Team Quebec at the Canada Games in 2007. Even as a teenager, Poulin could do things with the puck that no one else could. She was just special. Finally, Leclaire now thought, there's a league to give the best players in the world the spotlight they deserve, and thank goodness it came during Poulin's career.

Poulin is a magician with the puck, the type of player who can get you out of your seat. No one has been more consistent when it matters most on the ice than Poulin. She's one of the best to ever play the game. People have tuned in to see her every four years at the Olympics, and maybe once a year for the world championship. But she's had just as many magical moments wearing a Montréal sweater in the CWHL.

Poulin's big goals at the Olympics and world championships, sure, those are easy to find on the internet. But what about all the magic on past Montréal teams? Some of those games aired on low-quality streams. Some weren't broadcast at all and are lost forever. Poulin scored thirteen goals over two stints at the Under-18 Women's World Championship. Try to find a video of just one of those goals on the internet. You might need to call the FBI. It's sad to think of what's been lost, what we'll never get back.

Women's hockey has lacked visibility for years, but finally that's starting to change.

It's been a long time coming.

1
NOWHERE TO PLAY

Sami Jo Small was stunned when she read the email.

It arrived in her inbox on May 18, 2007, from the management of the Mississauga Aeros, the hockey team Small had played for over the last four seasons, to tell her that the National Women's Hockey League was suspending operations for the next season. One of the best goaltenders in the world, along with other top Canadian talent, suddenly had nowhere to play.

Small had played in the NWHL since 1999–2000, the league's second season, after Brampton Thunder founder Susan Fennell recruited her to play for her team. Small had already been to the Olympics and won a world championship by that point. She'd hoped to find a landing spot with an East Coast Hockey League or Southern Professional Hockey League team in men's hockey. When that didn't work out, she decided to take up Fennell's offer to play in Brampton, west of Toronto. When she arrived in town, Fennell, who would become Brampton's mayor in 2000, put Small up in a hotel. She got free goalie equipment for the first time in her life. Players had to find places to train on their own, but they got free gym passes, plus she had access to training as a member of Team Canada. The Brampton team played in what is now the CAA Centre in front of what Small felt were big crowds.

Brampton, by all accounts, was a "have" team in a league of haves and have-nots. But even the "have" teams, some of which offered perks like access to housing and a team's own dressing room, didn't pay women to play hockey. It wasn't uncommon for players across the league to drive to games in other cities in their own cars and to cover the costs of all their own equipment and meals. Most juggled all of this while working day jobs, which they had to do if they wanted to earn any money.

Small played for Brampton for two seasons. But after she returned from the 2002 Olympics, where she was a member of the gold-medal-winning Canadian team, Brampton Thunder signed other goaltenders. Small moved to the Toronto Aeros, a senior women's team with a rich history in the city. Then, in her fourth and final season with the Aeros, the team changed hands and relocated to Mississauga. With new owners she didn't know as well and who weren't in Mississauga, Small didn't have a sense of what was going on at a league level, which is why the news about the NWHL suspending operations caught her by surprise. It wasn't the first time female hockey players found themselves with nowhere to play, and it wouldn't be the last.

Women have been playing hockey since at least 1890. That's when a photograph was taken of a young Lady Isobel Stanley, dressed in a long, warm coat, playing hockey with friends on the frozen Rideau Canal. It's the earliest known photograph showing women playing the game and happens to depict a family synonymous with hockey in Canada. Lady Isobel's father, Lord Stanley, was Canada's governor general from 1888 to 1893, but he's probably best known for presenting the trophy that would be given to Canada's top men's hockey team and is now the holy grail in the NHL.

As Brian McFarlane documented in *Proud Past, Bright Future: One Hundred Years of Canadian Women's Hockey*, women's teams appeared throughout Canada in the late 1890s and early 1900s, from blue-collar workers playing in Saint John, New Brunswick, to collegiate hockey in Montréal, to a burgeoning league in Medicine Hat, Alberta. His research found the first documented women's hockey league in Quebec in 1900, with three teams from Montréal, one from Quebec City, and a fifth from Trois-Rivières. In the early days, McFarlane wrote, many of the women's games happened in private without spectators—definitely without men watching from the stands—and without much recognition or fanfare.

That seemed to be changing by 1922, when the powerhouse Ottawa Alerts hockey team played a home-and-home series with a Toronto team. They drew four thousand fans who loved the heavy-checking style of play on the ice, McFarlane wrote, and the games were covered in the *Toronto Star.*

The most dominant team of all may have been the Preston Rivulettes, a team from the small community of Preston, Ontario. During the 1930s, they racked up four national titles, ten provincial titles, and five Eastern Canadian championships, led by their captain, speedy Hilda Ranscombe. Along the way, the team often drew more spectators than men's teams, but they still found themselves with worse ice times, forced to accommodate men. The team only lost one game out of more than three hundred played, according to the Cambridge Sports Hall of Fame. They disbanded at the end of the decade when the Second World War began. The Cambridge Hall inducted them in 1997, and Canada's Sports Hall of Fame followed suit in 2022.

Some of the stories of Ranscombe and the Rivulettes have lived on, thanks to the Cambridge Sports Hall of Fame, the newspapers that documented those games, and historians like McFarlane who brought those stories to life decades later. But no statistics exist to show the scale of a player like Ranscombe's career. We have no idea exactly how many goals she scored as she led the team to championship after championship. The same goes for Ottawa Alerts stars like Shirley Moulds and Eva Ault in the 1920s.

Meanwhile, the achievements of the men who competed in the NHL, which was established in 1917, are detailed in the statistics kept during that same era. Just as the Rivulettes were dominating in the 1930s, men like Harvey (Busher) Jackson and Charlie Conacher were doing the same in the NHL. We can't put exact figures on just how prolific a player like Ranscombe was, but we know Conacher scored 345 points over 376 games during that decade. He was inducted into the Hockey Hall of Fame in 1961.

Because women's accomplishments in the sport weren't nearly as well documented, men's accomplishments in the sport have gotten significantly more recognition. While Jackson and Conacher are in the Hockey Hall of Fame, Ranscombe, Ault, and Moulds are not. It wasn't until 2010 that any woman was inducted into the hall. As of this writing, only twelve women have been selected.

More women's hockey was preserved heading into the 1980s and 1990s as the sport grew. The passing of Title IX in the United States, banning sex-based discrimination in collegiate sports, opened up the doors for more women to play NCAA (National Collegiate Athletic Association) hockey. The first world championship was held in 1990, and eight years later, women's hockey made its debut at the Olympics. That same season, the NWHL, where Sami Jo Small would play, was created. The NWHL, replacing the Central Ontario Women's Hockey League (COWHL) that existed before it, had teams in Ontario and Quebec that first season, all of which were privately owned.

The NWHL was home to many of the best players, but the teams relied on volunteers to operate. Back then, those volunteers did just about everything needed to help the team, sometimes even assisting on the ice. The games wouldn't have happened without them. Richard Scott was one of those volunteers. Scott, a self-described hockey nerd, volunteered for the Ottawa Raiders. Volunteering allowed Scott to blend his love for hockey with his experience working in magazines and dabbling in photography. It also meant he got a front-row seat to a lot of great hockey. He remembers one game in Toronto where more Olympians were on the ice than spectators in the stands.

In the 2006–07 season, which ended up being the NWHL's final one, Scott found himself compiling the league's statistics after learning there wasn't a model in place to do so. He hurried to make sure all the game sheets from across the league that season were sent to him. But there were holes. Sometimes the game sheets weren't filled out the same way. Goaltenders' statistics were tracked differently across the league. And in the case of ten games, the game sheets were nowhere to be found. That didn't just mean that a player's stat line was incomplete. Scott believed statistics were a way into telling the story of a league and its players. Missing game sheets meant a part of the NWHL's story was, and might always be, missing.

Scott also went back to compile statistics from leagues like the COWHL. There were also statistics from the Abby Hoffman Cup, awarded as a national women's championship in Canada beginning in 1982. But Scott found that game-by-game records didn't exist for at least the first decade of that championship, a sign of just how many holes existed even in the modern era. Even more recently, when leagues had folded, their websites had disappeared. Gone with them were pieces of those leagues' stories.

When the NWHL folded and a new entity, the CWHL, replaced it, Scott, still a volunteer, vowed to do things differently. "There was so much history that was lost with the NWHL in terms of some of the stats," Scott said in an interview in 2024, nearly two decades into his work preserving women's hockey history. "I was committed to make sure that, from a pioneering level, we would have this history from day one, that everything they did in that first season would be captured." As the CWHL grew, that task would transition from Scott's own spreadsheets to the hands of a Montréal volunteer named Valerie Nantel, who would spend hours rewatching games to make sure the league's records were accurate.

The stats Scott and Nantel compiled showed that Jennifer Botterill was the top scorer in the CWHL's inaugural season, logging sixty-one points in twenty-six games with Mississauga. But as a way to tell a story with those stats, Scott decided to create a trophy to honour the league's top scorer. There were a number of significant people in the game he could name it for. With the help of Small, he chose Angela James, the superstar who led Canada to gold at the first Women's World Championship in 1990. The Angela James Bowl was born. It briefly lived in Scott's basement before the league had a proper office. The winner each year would get their name on the big trophy and a miniature version to keep. For Scott, it was about more than a trophy. It was about preserving the story of the league.

Creating the Angela James Bowl would lead Scott to another project: publishing an annual *Who's Who in Women's Hockey Guide*. Each year's guide includes historical statistics for every woman who has played elite hockey dating back to the 1980s, plus the most recent stats for current players. The version Scott released in 2024 includes statistics for more than 3,900 players. He also published a complete CWHL record book after that league folded, preserving twelve years of its history. Some of Scott's commitment to these projects comes from his passion for publishing and collectibles and his love of hockey—his home bookshelves, built by his son, are stacked with hockey books. But mostly his work stems from a love of storytelling and a deep desire to make sure that history survives.

Sadly, in the many leagues and teams in the decades before, scattered across the country, much has been lost to time. "You just hope that you've got some more hockey nerds like me that are going to go backwards and try to put some of these stories together," Scott said.

The lack of documentation and preservation is an example of how women's labour in hockey has never been valued the same as men's. Even though women have been playing and excelling at the sport for more than a century, women have still had to fight for opportunities to play, let alone to be compensated and recognized for their achievements. That's why, when the NWHL folded, the players had to take matters into their own hands to keep playing the game they loved. And that's how the CWHL was born.

The email that Small and other players received in May 2007 indicated the NWHL would use the next season to restructure, but as the summer went on, information was hard to come by.

Small trained during the off-season with a number of Team Canada teammates in Scarborough, including some who had played on other NWHL teams. They didn't know what was going on either. With ownership groups dissolved, they weren't sure where to look for answers. Eventually, the group decided to hold a meeting at a pub in Scarborough, extending the invitation to some non–national-team players, too. They figured that getting everyone in one place would make it easier to figure out what was what. They also needed to make a plan for the next season, which was fast approaching. Always one to step up and try to solve a problem, Small knew the players would have to come up with a solution if they wanted a place to play. "How are we going to be able to play? I think that was just the real impetus. We simply wanted to play the next year," Small recalled in an interview.

A turning point came when NWHL goaltender Mandy Cronin met Toronto businessman Michael Salamon at a road-hockey tournament. She told him what was happening, and Salamon, a partner at a private equity firm called Birch Hill Equity Partners, decided he wanted to help. A group of players met with Salamon and some of his colleagues in Toronto. Reps from teams in Ottawa and Montréal phoned in. Salamon listened, and then he asked questions: "What do you guys want? What can we do to help? How can we move this forward?" The players told Salamon and his team that they wanted to create a league in time for the beginning of the next season so they could keep playing. And so the work began. Salamon and his colleagues offered help with the business side of setting up a new league, from offering legal assistance to helping write a business plan.

The league's founders had a long to-do list and not much time to complete it. Representatives from each team trekked to weekly meetings at Birch Hill Equity's downtown Toronto office to sort out things like booking ice and figuring out which ownership groups had left behind equipment like skate-sharpening machines and even pucks. They had to create a schedule, book travel, and find officials. Some teams had volunteer staff members left over from the NWHL, but others didn't.

The players decided that a board of governors, rather than individual owners, would run the new league and that it would be called the Canadian Women's Hockey League (CWHL). This structure meant every team would have the same resources, lessening the have-and-have-not divide that existed in the previous league.

At the beginning, sponsorships and donations would fund the league, with plans to expand revenue through ticket sales, marketing rights, and media. The organizers of the new league applied for Registered Canadian Amateur Athletic Association status, which allowed people to donate money to the league and receive a tax receipt. The players wouldn't be paid, but they hadn't been paid in the old league, either. "Although the CWHL players train tirelessly and represent many of the best female hockey players in the world, the players retain unpaid amateur status," a business plan submitted to the Canada Revenue Agency in 2007 stated. It was *professional hockey*, but that word had become a bit of a misnomer over the years. It was professional—as in high calibre—on the ice, in that many of the best players in the world played in the CWHL. But they wouldn't be considered employees or compensated for their work like many male "professional athletes" in leagues like the NHL, meaning they weren't exactly treated equally.

Sami Jo Small (right) during a game for the Mississauga Chiefs in 2008, during the CWHL's inaugural season. (Richard Scott)

The CWHL began play in September 2007 with seven teams, many of which were carried over from the NWHL: Brampton, Burlington, Ottawa, Montréal, Quebec City (which also played in Montréal), Vaughan, and Mississauga. Each team was associated with a girls' hockey association, and each team played thirty games in that first season. Sami Jo Small played for the Mississauga team.

At first, the league was supposed to be a stopgap measure so players would have a place to play. As time went on, it grew into more than that. But there were bumps along the way, especially in the early years. In November 2007, the Brampton Thunder travelled to Montréal for a game against the Montréal Stars. When they got there, according to coverage in the *Brampton Guardian*, they discovered no referees had been assigned to the game. Instead of cancelling the game, they appointed a player from each team to act as an official. The Stars won the game 3–2.

The Thunder won the first CWHL championship, and that team's top scorer, Canadian national-team superstar Jayna Hefford, was named the league's first MVP. Had Small and the other players not charted their own course, perhaps the best players wouldn't have had a championship to play for at all that season. And if that had happened, a sixteen-year-old phenom from a small city in Quebec might not have come to Montréal.

Instead, that fall marked the creation of a new league and the beginning of the pro career of a player who would change women's hockey forever.

—

Isabelle Leclaire will never forget the first time she saw Marie-Philip Poulin play hockey.

It was 2007, and Leclaire was an assistant with Team Quebec's Canada Games team. The team was doing a flow drill to start practice, and one girl stood out from all the rest on the ice. The way she handled and passed the puck was so smooth. It was unlike anything Leclaire had ever seen from a fifteen-year-old. Leclaire turned to the team's head coach, Pierre Alain, who was standing beside her. "Hey, look at that." She pointed to Poulin. "Who's that?"

They didn't know the young woman well. They scanned their list, eventually locating Poulin's name, and saw she'd been playing with boys back home in Beauceville. She was five years old when her parents saw how passionate their daughter was when she sat between them in the stands of an old community arena, watching her older brother, Pier-Alexandre, play. Not many girls played hockey at the time, but Poulin knew immediately that she loved the game.

They couldn't have known then that this would be the spark of a passion that would take their daughter to four Olympic Games, or that she would score the golden goal in three of those gold-medal games, something no one else, of any gender, has ever done. It would also take her to the big city of Montréal, where she would become the captain of the professional women's team. It would take her so far that when the city of Beauceville built a new arena to replace the old one where Poulin and her brother had played, they'd put up several large pictures of her on the outside of the rink as an homage, representing different stages of Poulin's career. There's Poulin wearing her Olympic medals around her neck and a Team Canada sweater, waving. In another, she's draped in a Canadian flag after winning gold in Sochi in 2014. They might have named the arena after her if Quebec didn't have a rule prohibiting naming places after people who are still alive.

The girl Leclaire met in 2007 was extremely shy and not yet able to speak much English. Leclaire watched her score seventeen points over five games for Quebec en route to a bronze medal at those Canada Games. But it's how Poulin handled a setback in the semifinals against a powerhouse Ontario team that lingers in Leclaire's mind, almost two decades later. As Leclaire remembers it, Poulin went for a loose puck and collided with Ontario's goaltender, who was diving toward the puck. Poulin was called for charging and given a game misconduct, meaning she was thrown out of that game and the next one, too. It was a massive loss for the Quebec team. Poulin was their best player.

It was Poulin's first tournament at a national level, and it must have been devastating for a teenager to watch her tournament end that way. But even if Poulin was sad not to finish the game, Leclaire remembers the teenager urging her team to keep going, telling them they could still do it without her. Quebec lost that game 3–1, felled by an Ontario team with several future Team Canada stars, including Natalie Spooner, Rebecca Johnston, and Brianne Jenner. Luckily for Team Quebec, Poulin's suspension was reversed in the next game after officials watched video of the play. She went on to record a goal and three assists in a 6–0 win over Saskatchewan for bronze.

A few months after her Canada Games debut, Patrick Rankine met Poulin for the first time. The general manager of the CWHL's Montréal Stars knew the girl was extremely talented. He wanted her to move to Montréal to play hockey against the best women in Canada. In a two-hour conversation with Poulin's parents, Rankine told them it would be better for Poulin to play at the highest level of women's hockey instead of elite boys' hockey. He was confident Poulin would play at the 2010 Olympics and would receive full scholarship offers from American universities. Learning English would be essential, and Montréal could help with that.

When they agreed, Rankine set out to find Poulin the right school and host family. They settled on Kuper Academy, where Poulin could study in English with the extra support of a Stars player who taught at the school. The school also had a hockey program, so Poulin could have extra time on the ice. She went to live with the Rougeau family, whom the Poulins knew because the Rougeaus' daughter, Lauriane, played alongside Poulin on Team Quebec. Like Poulin, Rougeau would go on to have a long hockey career that included winning an Olympic gold medal with Team Canada.

In one of her first games in the CWHL, Poulin registered five points in an 8–1 win over the Quebec Phenix. The next game, she scored her first hat trick, including the overtime game winner, in a 4–3 Montréal victory over Vaughan.

By Christmas, Poulin was leading the league's scoring race. But after missing nearly half the games that season while playing on other teams, including a stretch away on Canada's first women's under-18 world championship team and Quebec's under-18 team, Poulin wasn't able to hold the lead. But she finished that first season with forty-three points in only sixteen games and led the league in points per game (2.69). She was named the league's top rookie and finished second place in MVP voting, behind Jayna Hefford.

Poulin appeared in six CWHL seasons with the Montréal team, which was later renamed Les Canadiennes. She was named MVP in three of those seasons and helped Montréal win two championships. Beyond the championships, pulling on the Montréal jersey meant a lot to her because her hockey heroes, including Kim St-Pierre, Caroline Ouellette, and Lisa-Marie Breton, had also played for Montréal teams (in the NWHL).

With Poulin and other stars on the ice, the CWHL grew. The league hired its first commissioner, Brenda Andress, in 2008. By 2018, annual revenue had grown to more than $4 million. More games were broadcast. There were partnerships with NHL teams, though sometimes those associations gave the impression that the NHL was more involved than it was in funding the league. More than eight thousand people attended the CWHL All-Star Game at Toronto's Air Canada Centre (now Scotiabank Arena), in 2017. The league was making strides, and there was no doubt the quality of the play was good. But despite all its successes, over its twelve seasons the CWHL never became a place where players could make a living playing in the league.

2
THE DREAM GAP

Goaltender Liz Knox's alarm clock went off at five a.m. By seven, she was on a roof, where she'd spend the day lugging bundles of shingles back and forth, over and over, until it was time to quit. It was long, hard work, and Knox was exhausted by the time she climbed off the roof at suppertime.

Her day didn't end there. Knox had hockey practice twice a week, usually late at night because that was the only time her team could afford ice time. She didn't make it home until after midnight. Weekends were for playing games, usually two in two nights. Sometimes she travelled across Canada and back again in time for work on Monday morning.

It's the kind of routine a beer-league hockey player might have. But Knox didn't play in a beer league. She played for the CWHL's Brampton Thunder, which later became the Markham Thunder. The play on the ice certainly wasn't beer league. According to Richard Scott's *12 Seasons: The CWHL Records Book*, only two other goalies in CWHL history played more games than five-foot-four Knox, known as Knoxy to her teammates. It was an exhausting, unsustainable routine, and Knox kept it up until she was thirty years old. She did it because she loved the adrenaline rush she got when she made a big save and the mental focus it took to be at her best. But no matter how good Knox was, and no matter how many shots she stopped from national-team stars, playing hockey in the most competitive and elite league for women never paid her bills. She wasn't alone. During the CWHL's twelve-year existence, most of the players in the league worked other jobs. The CWHL did start paying its players in the 2017–18 season, but even then, players made as little as $2,000 per season, barely enough to cover the cost of their sticks. The more seasons Knox played in the CWHL, the more stark the divide became between players like herself, who worked full-time jobs, and the elite players who received enough funding playing for Team Canada to focus solely on hockey. Those who played on the national team could qualify for "carding" funding from the federal government and had their equipment and training costs covered by Hockey Canada. But with fewer than thirty players on the national team, that represented a small percentage of the women who played in the CWHL each season.

Over her years in the league, Knox heard many complaints from her teammates, all lamenting the lack of basic things: locker rooms, health benefits, even tape. In 2017–18, the league added two teams in China, an effort by the country to improve its calibre of women's hockey ahead of hosting the 2022 Winter Olympics in Beijing. It was a financial lifeline for the league, thanks to licensing agreements with the teams in China. Financial statements filed with the Canada Revenue Agency show the league's cash assets went from less than $60,000 in 2016 to more than $2 million in 2017, when the Chinese teams were added. However, it also meant each team made the trek across the globe to China once that season. The travel costs to China were covered by the league, but players like Knox, who worked other jobs, had to use up a week of vacation time. She came back to Toronto on a Sunday night and was back at her construction job the next day, still jet-lagged. She thought about how that kind of schedule wasn't one a regular person should keep, let alone an elite athlete. Worst of all, Knox said, players weren't consulted on the decision to add the extra travel to their schedules.

Fed up with feeling players were left out of decisions that affected them, Knox knew she had to do more to question why things were the way they were. "I thought, I can't just sit here and complain to my teammates about this," Knox said in a 2022 interview. "I have to be in the conversations about 'How did this happen? What is the expectation? What are we getting out of this?'" She became co-chair of the league's players' association. It was her job to take players' concerns to league management and to push for better conditions.

Knox was eight years old the first time she found herself questioning the status quo. Growing up in Stouffville, Ontario, a town north of Toronto, Knox came from a long line of figure skaters. But for as long as she can remember, hockey mesmerized her. Knox's grandfather ran a hockey camp in Sudbury, north of where Knox grew up, and she desperately wanted to attend. There was a little problem, though. There had never been a girl at the camp. "I really want to play," Knox said. "I don't care if it's all boys.'" Her grandfather agreed, and by the end of the two-week camp, Knox was hooked on the sport.

Growing up, Knox plastered her bedroom wall with posters of famous NHL goalies like Patrick Roy and Curtis Joseph. Until 2002, none of the posters showed women playing hockey. That year, when Knox was thirteen, the Canadian women's national team played in its second Winter Olympics and brought home the team's first gold medal. For some girls, it was the first time they'd seen women playing high-level hockey, and it would shape the dreams and directions of the female hockey superstars who came after them. After the Canadian women won gold, Knox's aunt gave her a poster of the team. "This could be you," her aunt wrote in permanent marker on the plastic wrap. Knox hung the poster over a light switch in her room. She saved the square her aunt wrote on and placed it over goaltender Kim St-Pierre. For the first time in her life, she had a female hockey-playing role model.

"I didn't know anything about them," Knox said later about the Olympians she watched on TV. "I just figured they played pro hockey their whole lives. You don't really ask those questions when you're a kid like, 'Where do they play in between? Why can't I watch them on TV?'"

Knox went on to a solid career in the Canadian university ranks. She played five seasons with the Wilfrid Laurier Golden Hawks, including one where she didn't lose a game until the last day of the season. She also got to pull on a Hockey Canada jersey and was part of the national-team program, but Knox would not follow in the footsteps of her 2002 heroes and make an Olympic team. For a player like Knox, there's no fanfare when your national-team career is over. They just stop calling.

When she reached the end of her university career, Knox had to decide what to do next. It's a common crossroads where some high-level female hockey players drop out of the game, as they're forced to choose between playing hockey and making a living. Knox had practised with the CWHL's Brampton Thunder in her final year of university and enjoyed it. She decided to enter the league's draft, and she put the Thunder as her first choice. It was a "draft" in name only, according to Knox, because players weren't drafted based on their ability alone. It wasn't realistic to expect a player to move across the country for a job that didn't pay. Instead, players were usually drafted by a team close to where they already lived, where they could work another job and play hockey on the side. Knox knew all of this when she entered the draft. She wasn't expecting to make money. She saw it as a way to keep playing the game she loved. "If you're playing hockey after university, that's why you're playing, because you just love being on a team and you love showing up to the rink and playing hockey," Knox said. "We never had a delusion going into the CWHL that it was going to be this professional experience."

In 2011, Knox's first full season with the Thunder, men playing in the NHL made a minimum salary of $500,000. In the American Hockey League, a tier below the NHL, players made at least $39,000. Knox made nothing. She actually paid out of her own pocket to play the highest level of women's hockey that first season. Knox said CWHL players were supposed to bring in $1,500 of sponsorship money as a registration fee. She felt strange asking businesses to sponsor her as an adult, so she paid the fee herself.

Later that season, the team's general manager wanted her to get new pads. Knox was still using purple gear from her time playing at Laurier, and it didn't match the Thunder's white-and-black jerseys. The manager printed out design sheets that Knox used to customize the set of new pads. She settled on red and white Vaughan gear, thinking the colours were subtle enough that she could keep using them if she found herself on a different team in the future. When she pulled on her new gear a few weeks later, Knox was elated. A couple of days after that, the team was practising on one of the rinks within the Cassie Campbell Community Centre, a community facility in Brampton. As Knox started to carry her equipment out of the locker room, her general manager stopped her to hand her a piece of paper. It was an invoice for her new gear. The total? Three thousand, five hundred dollars.

Knox was stunned. Even though she was playing in the highest tier of women's professional hockey in North America, there wasn't even a discount. She was expected to pay her own way, something men in the NHL wouldn't dream of having to do. Fresh out of university,

Knox had two part-time jobs, one at a Nike outlet and the other at a Lululemon store. Finding $3,500 on top of the $1,500 she'd already shelled out at the beginning of the season was a tough ask. But she didn't know what else to do. She borrowed the money from her parents and paid the bill. "I was so angry," Knox reflected on getting the bill. "But then I also felt a kind of imposter syndrome, honestly. Because I was like, [my teammates] are all pro hockey players. Who am I going to complain to? In a weird way, it was like, well, I guess this is just how it is because nobody seems to have a problem."

The most Knox ever remembers making in her CWHL career was $6,000 in 2017–18, the season the Thunder won the Clarkson Cup, the CWHL's championship trophy. That was the first season the CWHL started compensating players, after a rival American league began luring players away by offering salaries. Knox added up the money she had spent playing hockey that season, and she was in the red. Still, $6,000 felt like a nice bonus.

Not only did the job of a professional female hockey player not pay at a professional level in the CWHL, but many thought it didn't feel professional beyond the play on the ice. NHL teams are often the anchor tenant of massive rinks. In the CWHL, Knox played at community rinks where the best female hockey players in Canada shared space with minor hockey teams and beer league grinders. She remembers one CWHL game ending with two minutes left on the clock. It was nine p.m. and their rental was up, so their game was over. Two men's beer league teams were waiting to take the ice.

It's all part of what Knox describes as a dream gap—the gap between girls' hockey dreams and boys' hockey dreams. Boys can dream of being one of hundreds of players who suit up in the NHL each year, making, at minimum, hundreds of thousands of dollars. And if not the NHL, they can dream of playing in the American Hockey

League or the East Coast Hockey League or in any number of professional leagues in Europe.

Growing up, Knox never dreamed of playing professional women's hockey. She dreamed of making saves for the Toronto Maple Leafs, because that's who she watched on television every Saturday night. She dreamed of the NHL, where only one woman—goaltender Manon Rhéaume—has ever played, suiting up for two pre-season games in 1992 and 1993. The only hockey dream Knox could grasp, where players looked like her, was to play on the Olympic team, a dream only about two dozen women in Canada will achieve every four years.

The sense of unfairness ate away at Knox when she was eight, desperately wanting to be included in her grandfather's hockey camp. It ate away at her throughout her professional hockey career, as she burned both ends of the candle to play a game she loved. It ate away at her when she heard players talk about how desperately they wanted basic things.

Those same conversations had been happening within the women's American national team for years. A couple of years before the CWHL folded, their frustration came to a head, too.

As American forward Kendall Coyne Schofield describes in her book *As Fast As Her*, during her time on the national team, men and boys within USA Hockey received far more support than their female counterparts, from the support staff that worked with them, the travel and accommodations they received at tournaments, and the grassroots infrastructure, all the way down to how quickly championship rings were received for winning major tournaments. Coyne Schofield and her teammates were expected to train full time to maintain their spots on the national team, but they also had to find time to work second jobs to support themselves on top of that. And unlike men, none of them made enough of a living playing for a pro team to supplement the funding they received through USA Hockey. Simply put, they were tired of it.

In 2016, several leaders on the US national team began working with a lawyer named John Langel and the rest of the legal team at the firm Ballard Spahr to fight for better conditions within USA Hockey. Looking down the road, the team had a major piece of leverage—the 2017 Women's World Championship was going to be held on home soil in Plymouth, Michigan. If the women couldn't reach an agreement before then, they could refuse to play in the tournament. "It's sort of this collective thought like, 'Why not us?'" American forward Hilary Knight said in a 2022 interview. "'Why not now? If not us, then who?' We're just going to pass this to the next generation."

That idea of banding together to fight for something better for the next generation was inspired by a woman who did the very same thing decades earlier, at a time when women had even less power in sports and society at large: Billie Jean King. A staunch advocate for equality and social justice and one of the best tennis players of all time, King was fed up with making less than the best male players during her career. She used her status as a top-ranked player to fight for equal pay for female tennis players, banding together with eight other top female players in 1970 to boycott mainstream tennis championships, instead establishing their own independent women's Virginia Slims Circuit and signing token one-dollar contracts to protest the disparity in pay. The group would become known as the Original 9.

King led the formation of the Women's Tennis Association, and she successfully lobbied for equal prize money for male and female winners of the US Open in 1973. That same year, King defeated retired tennis pro Bobby Riggs in the legendary Battle of the Sexes match, which drew an estimated ninety million viewers across the world.

Two decades later, Team USA soccer player Julie Foudy met King at a roundtable event where she talked about signing the one-dollar contract and the courage it took for the women to take that risk. While she was listening to King's story, Foudy thought, *my God, this is all the same stuff we're fighting.* Speaking to King later, Foudy told her she hadn't realized how much her story mirrored the challenges the best female soccer players in America were having with their federation. King turned to her. "What are you doing about it, Foudy?" she asked. Foudy explained that they'd gone to the US Soccer Federation to ask for more. But King convinced her the players could be doing even more than that. "She used to always say, 'Imagine you have a blank canvas. It's not what you want for you, it's what you're building for the next generation. How do you leave this sport better?' It's how she's always thought about things," Foudy said in an interview

That group of American women, who won the Women's World Cup in soccer in 1999, became known for more than their exploits on the field. They also began a journey of fighting the federation for better treatment. As Caitlin Murray wrote in *The National Team: The Inside Story of the Women Who Changed Soccer*, just a year before winning the World Cup, the women had to get their lawyer, Langel—the same person who would help the American female hockey players years later—to fight for a bonus-payment structure equal to what the men had. Men had better accommodations, better food, better everything, on top of getting bonus payments for any medal won. The women, Murray wrote, would only get a bonus if they won gold. The soccer players took a page from King's book when contract talks with the US Soccer Federation reached an impasse. The team used the leverage of withholding their labour ahead of major tournaments to get the federation's attention. It worked because the players stuck together.

"She really was the start of our team getting to equal pay," Foudy said about King. "It started back in our day as equitable pay, and then we passed that torch on to that next generation who kept fighting, as they should have. But she was really the start of it all."

Throughout the women's soccer team's battle with their federation, Foudy knew women's hockey was facing similar issues. She'd had conversations with friends like American hockey star Cammi Granato. But it wasn't until 2016 that a group of leaders on the US women's hockey team took the first step toward taking a stand. Not only did they use the same legal team as the soccer players, but they also looked to them, including Foudy, for guidance. "To have the strength of the soccer program—I always feel like we're kind of following them," Hilary Knight said in an interview in 2022. "They set the bar and we get to benefit off of a lot of the groundwork that they do."

Foudy advised them to make sure everyone was on the same page. That was the only reason why the soccer players had been so successful. "You can't have a separation of players where some are willing to play and others are not, and they can divide and conquer you all," Foudy said. "Yes, have the courage to make this change, but do it as a group and make sure everyone is on board."

As Foudy advised, the hockey players managed to get everyone on the same page, including college players who could be called to fill in for the striking national-team players. Over months, a group of leaders—Coyne Schofield and Knight among them—alongside their legal team at Ballard Spahr negotiated with USA Hockey. They were unified. When they failed to reach an agreement by March 2017, and with the world championship in Michigan only a couple of weeks away, the players issued a statement on social media that said they wouldn't play in the tournament "unless significant progress has been made on the year-long negotiations with USA Hockey over fair wages and equitable support." The statement described how the players were looking for equal treatment when it came to compensation, travel expenses, hotel accommodations, publicity and marketing, equipment, meals, and staffing, as well as equal support at the grassroots level for girls. "The goals of our requests are to achieve fair treatment from USA Hockey, to initiate the appropriate steps to correct the outlined issues, and to move forward with a shared goal of promoting and growing girls and women in our sport while representing the United States in future competitions, including the Women's World Championship."

The strategy worked. They signed a new deal with USA Hockey just a couple of days before the tournament began.

Knight said she'll never forget how it felt to step off the plane in Michigan, ready to compete in the world championship after reaching a deal. She felt the magnitude of what the players had accomplished. To top it off, the Americans brought home gold, defeating the Canadians 3–2 in overtime. The players felt invincible after that. "It taught us that a strong group of women that are willing to put things on the line to stand up for a greater future is going to be successful," Knight said.

Coyne Schofield and Knight had proved what players could do if they stuck together. They also had allies in King and her partner, Ilana Kloss. Not only had King set the stage decades earlier for what the players accomplished in their fight against USA Hockey in 2017, but she and Kloss would also become key advisers and catalysts in what the hockey players wanted to do next.

3
FOR THE GAME
March 2019

On March 24, 2019, the Calgary Inferno defeated Les Canadiennes de Montréal for the Clarkson Cup title. No one knew it would be the CWHL's final game or that the Inferno's players would be the last ones to have their names engraved on a band of the storied sterling silver cup. A few days later, Liz Knox's phone chimed to let her know an email had landed in her inbox, inviting her and other players to a meeting with CWHL leadership the next morning. Knox wasn't expecting big news. Some players thought the six-team league might be adding or losing a franchise. One team from China had pulled out the season before. Maybe the other Chinese team was leaving, too.

Knox felt the news would be even less significant than a team coming or going. She thought the players' association had made it clear to the league that players wanted to have a say in big decisions before they were made. She hadn't gotten wind of anything big, so she figured it must be good news. Perhaps the league had found a new sponsor. Knox felt things were turning a corner in 2018–19. The league's fanbase seemed to be growing, with bigger crowds watching their games. It was becoming easier for fans to watch games on TV. And although it wasn't much, the players had finally started being paid, beginning in the 2017–18 season.

The call with players the next day was short, but the message was clear: the league was shutting down in a few weeks. The CWHL's board had decided the league and the way it was structured weren't sustainable. Stunned players had lots of questions but no opportunity to ask them. The call was over minutes after it started. Sitting on a bed at her now-wife's parents' house during the call, Knox felt her stomach drop. It was devastating. "I wasn't quite at the point of being angry," she recalled in an interview a few years later. "I was just like, somebody has just taken away something so important to you. They took away our game."

The CWHL's final public statement, released a couple of months later, described how the league wasn't generating enough revenue to keep operating. Running the league required at least $5 to $6 million per year and closer to $10 million if they wanted to do it at a level the league's leadership felt would be more professional. Financial records show the league had expenses of about $4.2 million in 2017–18 and brought in a little more than $4.4 million. The statement also suggested that having two leagues, the CWHL and the five-team upstart National Women's Hockey League (separate from the Canadian NWHL from the 1990s and 2000s, the American NWHL later rebranded as the Premier Hockey Federation), fractured the sponsorship dollars available. Pressure had mounted over the past few seasons for the CWHL and NWHL to merge, and the CWHL found some businesses preferred to wait until "one league" was in place before committing money to one or the other.

The hardest part for Knox was thinking about the players who had played their final professional hockey game without knowing it and without having a chance to properly thank the hockey world for what it had given them. "I think when you only get joy, you don't get money from playing hockey, being robbed of that last moment of gratitude was the most hurtful part of the CWHL closing," she said.

American Hilary Knight had just finished her first full season with Les Canadiennes. The roster was stacked with stars, including Knight, Marie-Philip Poulin, Erin Ambrose, Emerance Maschmeyer, Mélodie Daoust, Lauriane Rougeau, Geneviève Lacasse, and Jill Saulnier. Their team lost in the final to the Inferno, with Poulin injured. It was disappointing, but it felt like the sky was the limit for Les Canadiennes in their next season.

After losing in the Clarkson Cup final, Knight had turned her attention to the world championship. She was at an American national-team camp in Long Island, New York, preparing to travel to Finland, when word of the player call reached her. Like Knox, Knight wasn't expecting bad news. "I'm thinking, it can only be something good," Knight recalled. "Why would they drop it right here, right now?"

Kendall Coyne Schofield was rooming with Knight at the US team's camp when Knight received the news. Coyne Schofield had never played in the CWHL, but she was curious about the call. Many American national-team players had their eyes on leaving the NWHL. Some planned to join the CWHL the next season in an attempt to bring the best players into one league. Knight stayed behind to take the call while Coyne Schofield went for breakfast. When she returned to their room and Knight told her the CWHL was going to fold, Coyne Schofield's jaw hit the floor. She asked Knight if she'd seen it coming. Like many in the league, Knight hadn't. Even though Coyne Schofield hadn't played in the league, she remembers feeling the pain for those players and for the women's game.

Later that day, Knight, Coyne Schofield, and the rest of the Americans began the long journey to Finland. They had to focus on trying to win a world championship, but it was hard not to be distracted by the bombshell news. With the CWHL no more, many of the players had no idea where they'd play next season. Knight had lost her employer and with it her ability to work in Canada. Coyne Schofield knew she didn't want to go back to the NWHL. She had just finished her first season of professional hockey with the league's Minnesota Whitecaps, but it didn't feel professional to her. Along with Team USA teammates Lee Stecklein and Hannah Brandt, Coyne Schofield was the team's highest-paid player, making $7,000 a season. The money wasn't enough, however, for her to move to Minnesota from her home in Palos Heights, Illinois, just outside Chicago. Instead, she flew in on weekends for games, crashing on an air mattress on the floor of Brandt's apartment. At the end of the weekend, she'd fly home and go back to work. It meant she never got to practise with her team. "It's not the way a team sport works," Coyne Schofield said of her year in the league. "So that was hard for me mentally. That's not the way that things should be done."

Knight had started her professional hockey career with the CWHL's Boston Blades in 2012. It had been a rude awakening coming from the University of Wisconsin, where players had everything they needed. As a professional in Boston, Knight got dressed on two upside-down milk crates because there wasn't enough seating for all the players in the dressing room they used. When she wasn't training or playing for the Blades, Knight offered private hockey lessons to try to make ends meet. She made friends with a guy who worked at Dunkin' Donuts who would give her the old bagels, cinnamon rolls, and doughnuts they were going to throw out at the end of the day. "Waking up every day trying to figure out where your next meal is coming from and things like that is serious for a lot of players," Knight said about those years. "When we want to put the best product on the ice, you can't be worrying about what other job you're going to do."

Knight had left the CWHL to play in the NWHL for two seasons and had been a face of the league in its early years. In 2016, during Knight's second season with the NWHL's Boston Pride, the league announced it was slashing player salaries in order to keep the league running. According to figures disclosed by the league that season, Knight had been set to earn $20,000 before salaries were slashed. In response, Knight and other players called for more transparency from the NWHL. They wanted to know the identity of investors and to see a third-party audit of the league's finances so they could understand how the league's financial picture had declined so dramatically during the season. They also wanted to see proof of insurance "to ensure that the players are not risking their health by playing and practising." That 2016–17 season would be Knight's final season in the NWHL and she ultimately went back to the CWHL. With the CWHL no longer an option, and neither wanting to play in the NWHL, both Knight and Coyne Schofield started to think about building something new.

The wheels were already in motion even before the American players' bus arrived at the airport en route to Finland. One of the first calls was to Billie Jean King and Ilana Kloss. The couple would become trusted advisers and key figures in what the players wanted to build.

When she boarded the plane, Knight paid for Wi-Fi. She knew she had to start rallying players, because if she'd learned one thing from King, and from the Americans' fight with USA Hockey in 2017, it was that strength would be in numbers. She knew people would immediately want to move to the NWHL, the last remaining women's hockey league in North America, but felt that wasn't necessarily the best move for the game as a whole.

Neither player had experience building a league from scratch, but they both had experience bringing people together from the battle with USA Hockey. But before things could go much further, the Americans had to do something they'd never done before during a world championship, something almost unimaginable to anyone who's watched two decades of blood, sweat, and tears in women's hockey: they had to sit down at the same table as the Canadians.

Few sports rivalries are as bitter as the one between Canada and America in women's hockey. In 2018, the Americans won their first Olympic gold medal in twenty years in a shootout. The Canadian players stood on the blue line, tears streaming down their faces as they received their silver medals. Four years before that, in a game leading up to the 2014 Olympics, the Canadian and American national teams got into a brawl on the ice. Ten players were penalized for fighting that day, including Knight. Some people think the rivalry between the United States and Canada has cooled over the years, as more players have competed together at college and become friends. That couldn't be further from the truth. But in the spring of 2019, these players felt their sport had reached a crossroads, and they needed to talk about what to do next. Leaders from the American and Canadian teams gathered together in the lobby of their hotel at a long table where players usually ate breakfast. Things were a bit awkward. "When we're in tournament, we're not meeting up," Knight said. "Sometimes people won't even ride the elevators together."

Even though they played for different flags, the players all had one thing in common: they all knew how it felt to pour every part of themselves into something they loved for little to no money, and what it was like to play in community rinks, dragging their equipment back and forth. Coyne Schofield remembered everyone at the table saying the same thing: we can't keep doing this. First, the Americans and Canadians had to play in a world championship, a task that would take all of their focus and energy. But they knew they were on the same page and that after the tournament ended, they had work to do together.

Like Knight, Coyne Schofield had the American team's victory in 2017 against USA Hockey fresh in her mind. She believed in what the players deserved. "As a group, we were going to have to fight for it," Coyne Schofield said in 2022, thinking back to that time. "No one was going to hand it to us. But we have a freakin' powerful group, a strong group, and the best group in the world to do this."

Days after news of the CWHL's demise, Liz Knox spoke with Kendall Coyne Schofield for the first time. The Americans wanted to bring all the players into a conversation to figure out how to move the women's game forward. Coyne Schofield was amazed at how unified players from the CWHL seemed to be. She asked if she could join one of the players' meetings, and Knox said yes. "Just being a fly on the wall at the time, I think it was a moment where I realized this group could come together, regardless of if you played in this league, that league, this national team, that national team," Coyne Schofield later said.

In the weeks after the CWHL folded, questions in the media swirled around whether players would flock to the NWHL. Within twenty-four hours of the CWHL's announcement, the NWHL's founder and commissioner, Dani Rylan Kearney, suggested her league wanted to fill the gap by expanding to Canada. "We will pursue all opportunities to ensure the best players in Canada have a place to play," Rylan Kearney said in a statement to Reuters and other news agencies. “Those conversations have started already and have quickly become a priority.” The eagerness to expand rubbed some players, like Knox, the wrong way. They were still digesting the loss of their league.

A little more than a month after the CWHL news broke, Knox was part of a group that sat down with the NWHL Players' Association. The CWHL players were armed with a list of questions. If they played in the league, would they have health benefits? Would they have professional facilities with locker rooms? Would they be paid, and if so, how much? Would they have to buy their own sticks and tape? If they were going to go to the NWHL, they wanted something better than they'd had with the CWHL, Knox said. “This is a fresh wound, and we don't want to have this same pain five years down the road,” she explained. “It wasn't that the NWHL wasn't good enough. It wasn't that all of a sudden we were going to make this stand for equality. It was, ‘We're hurt right now, and we don't want to be hurt again.’” They left the meeting with more questions than answers and feeling that playing in the NWHL would be no different than life in the CWHL. Some of the American national-team players had already reached the same conclusion. The state of women's professional hockey, Knox said, “was not what we wanted it to be.”

The group of players who were fed up—Knox, Coyne Schofield, and Hilary Knight among them—held an all-player meeting with anyone who was interested, including players from the NWHL. They asked who wanted to play in the NWHL, and who wanted to add their name to a list of women who wanted to build something new. They were drawing a line in the sand, just like the American players had done in their battle with USA Hockey in 2017. Soon after, the group decided to make a public statement. On May 2, 2019, more than two hundred female players vowed they would not play professional hockey until their labour was properly compensated. They wouldn't play in a league until they could do so in professional facilities and didn't have to drag their equipment home every day. "We cannot make a sustainable living playing in the current state of the professional game," the players wrote in a letter shared on social media with the hashtag #ForTheGame. "Having no health insurance and making as low as two thousand dollars a season means players can't adequately train and prepare to play at the highest level."

Even though the players had represented different leagues, teams, and countries in the past, the statement indicated they were all on board to fight for something better. "The time is now for this family to unite," they wrote. "This is the moment we've been waiting for—our moment to come together and say we deserve more. It's time for a long-term viable professional league that will showcase the greatest product of women's professional hockey in the world."

The players formed the Professional Women's Hockey Players Association (PWHPA). It wasn't a union yet. They didn't have an employer. But it was a labour movement, driven by women who felt their work wasn't properly valued. The ultimate goal was to build their own league on their terms—and for it to last. A board made up of players, which included Knox, Knight, and Coyne Schofield, drove that vision.

For now, the players knew they needed to stay on the ice, so they could both get their message out and keep playing. They began figuring out what that might look like in the fall of that year. There were a lot of issues to resolve. How would players be insured? Where would they be playing? Who would be playing? How would they sell tickets? How would they find officials and equipment managers? How would they find sponsors? "Some of us were also playing with the national teams and doing other jobs," Knight recalled, "so it was just this collection of women having to continue to pick up and keep marching forward."

The group needed a leader who could guide them where they wanted to go. They turned to a familiar face: Jayna Hefford. As a player, Hefford had led Team Canada to four consecutive Olympic gold medals, and has been one of the faces of women's hockey in this country. She grew up in Kingston, Ontario, idolizing Wayne Gretzky and dreaming of winning the Stanley Cup. Her hockey dreams changed in 1990, when twelve-year-old Hefford watched Canada win the first Women's World Championship. She made her debut with Team Canada at the world championship seven years later, and would write some of her own history in a Canadian jersey. In the final second of the middle period of the 2002 Olympic gold-medal game, Hefford scored what would be the game-winning goal, securing Canada's first Olympic title in women's hockey. Hefford retired from playing in 2015 and was inducted into the Hockey Hall of Fame in 2018. She ranked third on the CWHL's all-time goal scoring list with 130 goals, only two behind leader Noémie Marin and one behind second-place Caroline Ouellette.

Hefford had taken the reins as commissioner of the CWHL in 2018, and she had been the person who had to tell players that the CWHL was no more. She'd worked into June 2019 tying up the CWHL's loose ends, putting to bed a league that she had also loved as a player.

Hefford didn't immediately say yes when Coyne Schofield and Ilana Kloss phoned her in July 2019, asking her to become the players' association's operations consultant. "My first thought was, *Do I really want to do this?*" Hefford said in an interview a few years later. "*This has been difficult and hard and saddening and everything else that we all dealt with throughout that time. Do I really want to get back in this?*" The second question that ran through her mind was whether the PWHPA players really wanted her, the person who made difficult decisions and had delivered bad news in the CWHL just a couple months earlier, to lead them. "They said yes, this is what the players want," she said. "They need someone to come in, handle day-to-day operations, and guide this group."

After talking to her family and other people she trusted, Hefford decided to say yes. The deciding factor was that it was what the players wanted. Hefford wasn't very far removed from her own playing

Hilary Knight competes during the PWHPA's first Dream Gap Tour in 2019. (Richard Scott)

career and still felt she had a player's mindset, so it wouldn't be hard to work for them. She believed she could help because she understood what they needed and what they wanted. She, too, had played in the CWHL and the leagues that came before it, and no matter what she accomplished on the ice, Hefford never made any money playing in a pro league outside of her national-team career.

She started the job in August. Later that month, the association announced the Dream Gap Tour, which saw players make stops across North America, showcasing their play on the ice and trying to raise awareness for what they were working toward.

Volunteers and a handful of staff, including Hefford, powered them. The tour stopped in Toronto, New Hampshire, Chicago, Philadelphia, and Arizona that first season, drawing media attention for the players' decision to sit out of league play. Other games were held in San José, Boston, and Laval, Quebec. A tour stop in Japan was set for March 2020 but was cancelled due to the COVID-19 pandemic. That's something organizers couldn't have predicted when they planned the Dream Gap Tour. Players thought they might be out of a league for only one season. But for months into the pandemic, as the NHL resumed play, the best female hockey players in the world were off the ice, and their goal seemed far away.

4
THE VERDUN AUDITORIUM
October 2022
Montréal, Quebec

The ice inside Montréal's Verdun Auditorium was almost empty when a Team Sonnet trainer tossed a black milk crate over the boards. Iya Gavrilova, a three-time Olympian with Team Russia and a forward on Team Sonnet, grabbed the crate and slid it toward the net. Her teammate, Hilary Knight, stickhandled a puck down the ice before flipping it into the crate. With fifteen minutes to go before their game was to begin, Gavrilova, Knight, and defender Erin Ambrose were collecting the pucks from warm-up and putting them back in the crate. At the other end of the ice, Team Scotiabank teammates Mélodie Daoust and Alex Carpenter were doing the same thing.

In the NHL, superstars like Auston Matthews and Connor McDavid aren't picking up their own pucks after warm-up. Arena staff come out to clean after the players are done. But women's hockey has always been different. On the PWHPA tour, the players put the pucks away. They also planned their own tour stops. On this October Saturday, when the leaves had turned but the weather outside still felt sunny and warm, Montréal was the first stop on the players' barnstorming 2022–23 Secret Dream Gap Tour—named that way not because it was a secret but because the deodorant brand served as a title sponsor.

The Verdun Auditorium, their home that weekend, first opened its doors in the borough of Verdun in southwest Montréal in 1939. Two years later, British flags replaced the banners celebrating title-winning teams when the arena was transformed into a makeshift home for Canadian soldiers training for war. A few reminders of that era remain inside the rink, including the slatted wooden benches for spectators. They're mixed with modern touches. Over the last few years, the Verdun Auditorium was renovated to house Centre 21.02, a training centre for elite female hockey players in Quebec. It's named for February 21, 2002, the date the Canadian women won their first-ever gold medal at the 2002 Winter Olympics, changing women's hockey in Canada forever.

The centre was the brainchild of Danièle Sauvageau, women's hockey legend and head coach of that historic 2002 team. She wanted to create a place where women could be treated as professionals, with everything they needed in one place. The goal was to create a hub to develop the best players in Quebec. But elite female players with no connection to the province have also moved to Montréal just to train at Centre 21.02. It was a lifeline to players during the pandemic after Sauvageau and the centre secured permission from the Quebec government to keep national-team players on the ice. The PWHPA hadn't created the league the players envisioned yet, but the centre was created with that league in mind.

Throughout the 2022–23 season, PWHPA players travelled across North America, playing weekend showcases, running skills sessions, and signing autographs. Some did it on top of commitments with the Canadian or American national teams. Others did it in between working full-time jobs as firefighters, nurses, and teachers, to name a few. Some used their vacation time to travel to the showcases, flying across the continent and then back to work on Monday mornings after playing two or three games.

The games in Montréal on that weekend were the beginning of a season that felt like normal for the first time since 2020. There weren't any COVID-19 restrictions that prohibited players from crossing the border or limitations on the number of fans in the stands, and all the national-team stars were back in the fold after a season away. A few months earlier, the Canadians had won Olympic gold after players went through months of COVID tests and isolation in hotels to make it inside China's Olympic bubble.

In previous PWHPA seasons, players primarily trained at several hubs across North America in cities like Montréal, Toronto, and Minnesota. COVID-19 restrictions had made travel across the border difficult for the previous two years, and games were hard to come by. But this season, instead of competing on a team with the players they trained with in their hub, the players were mixed up into four teams meant to be evenly divided by skill. Each team was named after a sponsor—Adidas, Harvey's, Sonnet, or Scotiabank. It meant Americans and Canadians who had never played together before were suddenly teammates, a hint of what a future pro league would look like. Teams accumulated points at every tour stop, which determined their seeding for playoffs held at a championship showcase in the spring of 2023. The winner got to hoist the Secret Cup, again named after the deodorant brand. The tour still wasn't a league, not what players had been sitting out to fight for since 2019, but it was the closest thing to a league environment these players had experienced in three years. After watching the CWHL disappear and a pandemic take them off the ice, getting a chance to compete wasn't something these players took lightly.

New sponsor logos dotted the boards at Verdun Auditorium, including CCM, which outfitted the players with equipment. For some, it was the first time since college that they'd gotten new sticks or skates that they hadn't had to buy themselves. For players who spent years hoping not to break an expensive stick, it felt like their fortunes were finally turning. Another sponsor was Gatorade, a company that had recently decided to drop its NHL sponsorship to focus more on women's sports—something that would have been unthinkable back in 2019, when the CWHL folded. Canadian Tire also signed on. Earlier in October, that company had cut ties with Hockey Canada as a result of a reckoning of men's hockey culture stemming from sexual assault allegations against some men on the 2018 world junior team. The company committed to spending a minimum of 50 per cent of its sponsorship dollars on women's professional sports by 2026.

Fans flocked to the auditorium's wooden seats on the first day of the showcase, although the place wasn't filled to its capacity of a little more than 3,200 people. At the top of the stands on one side, inside a media booth, sat Jared Book, a journalist who's covered women's hockey in Montréal since 2005. A few days earlier, the PWHPA had asked Book to do the play-by-play for the broadcast streamed on YouTube and the CBC Sports website. It felt like a return to normal for Book, too, reminiscent of the days when he covered some of these players in the CWHL for the Habs Eyes on the Prize website.

No one knew when the PWHPA would finally announce the league they'd been working toward since 2019, but there was never any doubt that Montréal would be a part of it.

And this building was always meant to be its home.

—

Women's hockey has roots in Montréal dating back to McGill University in the 1890s. Back then, according to Brian McFarlane's research in *Proud Past, Bright Future: One Hundred Years of Canadian Women's Hockey*, women played for four hours each week, and men weren't allowed to attend and watch, except for the officials and those who guarded the entrances, making sure everyone followed the rules. In the 1920s, the Quebec Ladies' Hockey Association competed for the Lady Meredith Cup. By the 1980s and 1990s, stars like France St-Louis, who didn't yet have a big stage where she could shine for Team Canada, played in the Ligue régionale de hockey au féminin.

Quebec was a big part of the Canadian NWHL when it began in 1998. Of the three Quebec-based teams in that league, the one that would last the longest was created in 1998 as the Montréal/Bonaventure Wingstar. They became the Montréal Axion in 2003. The ashes of that team turned into the Montréal Stars when the NWHL folded and the CWHL replaced it. After a partnership was formed with the NHL's Montréal Canadiens, the team changed its name to Les Canadiennes de Montréal in 2015. Many of the women who played on those teams were already familiar to fans in Montréal by the time they became professionals, whether it was from playing university hockey at McGill or Concordia or from their earlier years in CEGEP, the publicly funded colleges unique to Quebec's education system. Before Kim St-Pierre won three straight gold medals as part of Team Canada, and before she played professionally in Montréal, she'd backstopped the McGill University Martlets.

That's also how Book fell in love with women's hockey. Book was working for *The Concordian*, a Concordia University student newspaper, in 2005. One day, the paper was set to go to production, but it still didn't have a cover story. The women's hockey team was donating proceeds from a tournament to a relief fund for people affected by the Indian Ocean earthquake and tsunami that had happened a few months earlier, so Book's editor sent him to speak to the team's head coach, Les Lawton. Book interviewed Lawton and really liked him. Book had only ever covered one women's hockey game, but Lawton welcomed him. He decided women's hockey was going to be his new beat, though it would take a month or two longer for Book, who was shy, to get the courage to interview players. Even though he was in the women's hockey world through university hockey, he still didn't know much about the professional women's hockey scene in the city.

It wasn't until 2014 that Book found himself covering the Montréal women's pro team, which was still called the Stars then. Players had just returned from the Olympics in Russia, and the team held a press conference to welcome them back. Book had been out of university for a little while and was looking for a way back into journalism and the joy he'd found writing about women's hockey at Concordia. He went to the press conference, spoke to Stars players like Caroline Ouellette and Julie Chu about their Olympic experiences, and never looked back.

A strong group of twenty to thirty volunteers from the community bolstered the CWHL team in those years. Book realized when he went to other CWHL markets that the combination of a strong volunteer base and a community that watched players grow up in front of them created a passion for women's hockey in the city. Not every team had someone who handled media requests, nor did every team have as many fans in the stands as Montréal attracted. As Book covered the sport, he saw how many players' pathways went through Montréal, even if they had no connection to the city. "I always say, you can't write about women's hockey history without mentioning Montréal," Book said in a 2024 interview.

After the star-studded Les Canadiennes lost in the CWHL playoffs in 2019, Book felt a championship could be within reach the next season, if only the team could avoid having so many significant injuries. Just like the players, Book was shocked when he was sitting on his couch, scanning social media, and learned the CWHL wouldn't have another season. The best women's hockey team he'd covered was no more, just when he'd felt everything was turning a corner.

Covering that league wasn't always easy. Book remembers attending one league awards gala in Ottawa where no plans had been made for journalists to watch the gala up close. Instead, reporters were

Karell Émard and Marie-Philip Poulin pose with the Clarkson Cup as CWHL champions with Les Canadiennes in 2017—one chapter in a long history of women's hockey in Montréal. (Richard Scott)

banished to a dressing room to watch the awards show on a small TV. Getting information like a lineup before a game was a luxury. Book even covered one game where the Montréal team and the Markham Thunder both packed their white jerseys. The Thunder ended up wearing jerseys from a junior team in Brossard. Book saw it all as a product of the league not having resources.

But his city's passion for women's hockey and the many familiar faces he would see at games kept Book carving out time and spending his own money to cover the sport. It was never about making money for him, let alone making a living wage covering the sport. No one who covered the CWHL or the leagues that came before it were in it for the money. It was the community that drove Book back to the Verdun Auditorium in October 2022. Walking around the media room and seeing familiar faces roaming around the rink felt like coming home.

On the last day of the Montréal showcase, Lindsay Browning was juggling—literally. She'd spent the last year trying to get the hang of juggling four balls, but on this day, she kept three in the air. Juggling before a game helped Browning wake her eyes up, and before her professional hockey debut, it helped the Team Sonnet goaltender calm her nerves. When she noticed people watching her routine inside the rink, Browning got freaked out and moved to a more private area. "This feels like a once-in-a-lifetime opportunity to be able to play in [the PWHPA]," Browning said that day.

A few months earlier, after graduating from Cornell University with a master's degree in biomedical engineering, Browning had thought her hockey career was over. Women have few opportunities to keep playing after college, and goaltenders even fewer. "It was probably the most upset I've ever been in my life," Browning said of that first month without hockey. “It’s in your blood. Once you’re a hockey player and you’re competitive, you can never get it out of you.” Soon after, she found herself on the ice for a pickup game in her home state of New York. She decided she wasn’t ready to give the sport up yet. She tried out for the PWHPA in Boston, and she made one of the four teams. She was doing cancer research at Harvard University by day and holding onto her hockey dreams in her spare time.

Before her first game began in Montréal against Team Harvey’s, Browning crouched low in her crease. She skated from post to post, tapping each one. She held her own in the game, saving a breakaway chance less than three minutes in. When the game went to three-on-three overtime, tied 2–2, she made a glove save on a dangerous shot from Team Harvey’s forward Emily Clark. Then came a shootout. Team Harvey’s won a coin toss and sent out Marie-Philip Poulin to take the first shot. Since they toured across North America, PWHPA teams didn’t have home rinks. But Verdun Auditorium was as close to home ice as Poulin could get. The crowd was on her side. *Oh crap*, Browning thought. *What am I going to do here?*

Browning tapped the left post with her glove as Poulin took off with the puck on her stick, connecting with the tape Poulin applies before every practice, every game, and sometimes in between periods: all the way down the blade, cut at the corner, with space left at the tip, and unscented stick wax. Poulin came in with speed, and Browning thought she was going to put the puck high. She didn’t. Poulin deked Browning to the right of her net and easily tapped the puck in on her backhand, just before Browning could get a glove in the way.

Browning kept her team in the shootout with a couple more saves, but Team Harvey’s won the game. Browning was named second star of the game after making thirty-three saves, a formidable performance in her first professional start.

Inside the media room after the game, Poulin finished an interview and tapped Browning on the shoulder.

"Good game," Poulin said.

"That was stressful," Browning responded, drawing a laugh from the veteran. "She deked me out of my socks," Browning told a reporter after her interaction with Poulin. "It almost feels like an honour to be dangled. And next time I'll get her."

Poulin's job in October 2022 wasn't just to deke poor Lindsay Browning out of her socks. She also had to promote and advertise the game in a way the men in the NHL have never had to do, so the women could create something to give people like Browning, and not just the Poulins of the world, an opportunity to play the game at a professional level. She also had to take the extra time to meet kids at the rink and give them something to dream about, all while hoping the young players' futures would look very different than her present. "There were so many moments this weekend where you hear your name, you look back, and that smile and that spark in those eyes, it's just like, wow," Poulin said in an interview after the win over Team Sonnet. "It's just awesome to see." It was also a taste of what a future league could look like: national-team foes turned friends mixed across rosters, making for competitive hockey. By the end of the weekend, every one of the four teams had a win. For Poulin, it was a reminder of what she'd been missing these last few years. It had been a long time since she'd heard the roar of the Montréal crowd or got to see familiar faces in the stands. But it wouldn't be the last time. "We wanted the league yesterday," she said that weekend. "We're all aware of that. But every big thing takes patience, and we know it's going to happen, and it's going to be viable and sustainable for a long time."

—

While the PWHPA's barnstorming North American tour stopped in cities that could someday be home to a team in a pro league, teams also went to places that you might not associate with elite women's hockey. The town of Truro, Nova Scotia, would probably fall into that category. With its population of fewer than thirteen thousand people as of 2021, it can sometimes feel like more deer are roaming the town's streets than people. But for the second year in a row, Truro was part of the PWHPA's North American tour schedule. The players set up camp inside the Rath Eastlink Community Centre for three days in November 2022, playing on an NHL-sized rink that's normally home to a men's junior-A team.

For a few people, the weekend was a homecoming. Team Harvey's head coach Kori Cheverie grew up a short drive away in New Glasgow, charting a path from her small town all the way to playing for the Toronto Furies in the CWHL and then coaching in the PWHPA and with Team Canada. Players Blayre Turnbull and Jill Saulnier were also playing at home for the first time in many years. They should have had this moment in 2020, when Nova Scotia had been set to host the Women's World Championship, but the pandemic had put the brakes on that plan. Both sat alone in Nova Scotia hotels for two weeks in 2021 in an attempt to play the rescheduled tournament, only for COVID-related health concerns to force its cancellation at the last minute.

Now, a year later, they'd finally play in front of friends and family. Turnbull, who grew up in Stellarton, less than an hour's drive east of Truro, was on the ice in the first game of the showcase for Team Scotiabank against Team Sonnet, taking the ceremonial faceoff in front of the home crowd. In the second period, with her team trailing

1–0, Turnbull skated to the net and dropped a pass behind her, between two Sonnet players, to teammate Shannon Stewart. Stewart buried it to tie the game. Turnbull scored the second goal of the period, in what would end up being the game winner for Team Scotiabank. She looked up to see her cousins cheering along the glass. She was named first star of the game.

After it ended, a few of the players settled into a meeting room to sign autographs. A long line snaked out of the room onto the concourse, and many waited to meet Turnbull in particular. It was something the players did after every game in addition to running clinics in the places they visited. The autograph line that night included twelve-year-old Adison White, a Halifax player who was playing AAA hockey with boys that season. "She's so aggressive on the puck," White said of Turnbull. White's parents had let her stay up to watch Turnbull, Saulnier, and the rest of the Canadian team win gold at the Olympics the previous winter. It wasn't lost on her that two players from Nova Scotia made that team. "I find it makes me push harder to be able to show that I can also do that as a player," White said. The next day, Turnbull and Saulnier were on the ice with local girls, running drills.

After Turnbull's game, Saulnier and her Team Adidas played Team Harvey's, led by Saulnier's friend, Marie-Philip Poulin. This was the first year in a long time that Saulnier and Poulin had competed on different teams. In addition to playing together on the national team, Saulnier had played with Poulin in Montréal after a trade sent her to Les Canadiennes in the CWHL in 2018. Even though the CWHL didn't exist anymore, Saulnier was still living in Montréal to train at Centre 21.02 alongside Poulin and several other members of the national team, drawn to the resources available and the opportunity to train with players who could push her to become better. In previous years, PWHPA players who trained together had also played on teams together. But with everyone mixed up this year, Saulnier had to get used to facing off against Poulin again.

Their game finished tied 3–3, sending them to three-on-three overtime. It looked like it might be over a couple minutes in when Team Adidas forward Kristin O'Neill took off on a breakaway and tried to deke Team Harvey's goaltender Ann-Renée Desbiens. But Desbiens didn't give her any space. Poulin won the next faceoff, sending the puck back to American defender Lee Stecklein. She put the puck ahead to Poulin, and she was off. Poulin skated down the right side of the ice, carrying the puck end to end and weaving past an Adidas player. She kept control of the puck in front of the net and flicked it over Team Adidas goaltender Maddie Rooney for the overtime winner. Captain Clutch had done it again.

When Poulin scored, Saulnier couldn't help but giggle, even though she was on the losing end of it this time. "I'd put money on her in overtime," Saulnier said after the game. "I think a lot of us would." Like Turnbull, Saulnier had family in the stands; she'd spotted her grandparents in the crowd during warm-up, and her mother was seated behind the net. It was the first time the Halifax native had played a competitive game in her home province in about fifteen years. But even though she'd left Nova Scotia years ago to chase her hockey dreams, Saulnier's heart was still there.

Just four years earlier, Saulnier had walked into a Halifax hardware store with a broken silver medal in her purse, hoping to find something to glue it back together. She'd won the medal in 2018, when she and Turnbull became the first Nova Scotians to make the Canadian women's Olympic hockey team. It was an accomplishment, but it wasn't a happy ending. Saulnier had come home to Halifax feeling like she'd let her country down after the Canadians lost the gold medal to the Americans in a shootout.

To understand Saulnier and how she broke her silver medal, you need to understand the Maritimes. The degrees of separation in a place like Nova Scotia are few. Maybe you don't know everyone you meet, but you might know their cousin, or their aunt might have been your second-grade teacher. And if you don't know them, it doesn't really matter anyway. It's not hard to find a stranger to help change your flat tire or maybe even try to glue your Olympic medal back together.

That's what life was like on the homemade rink where Saulnier and her brother, Brennan, played growing up in the Westmount neighbourhood of Halifax. Their parents, Darren Saulnier and Christine Brennan, took shifts maintaining the ice. Darren was on duty during the day, and Christine would take over in the evening when Darren went to work. When he returned home around two a.m., he'd flood the rink so it would be ready for Jill and her brother to use when they woke up. Neighbourhood kids were always welcome on the rink they called Saulnier Pond. Skating around on the ice with her brother, Saulnier dreamed of playing for her favourite NHL team, the Montréal Canadiens. It wasn't until 2002, after watching the Canadian women's hockey team stand on the blue line and celebrate their country's first gold medal, that nine-year-old Saulnier's Olympic dreams took root. Two years later, she got another taste of her dream when the Women's World Championship was held in Halifax. Seeing women play live at just one tournament fuelled her dreams. But she didn't have a clear path to follow. Until Saulnier and Turnbull did it in 2018, a Nova Scotian had never been on the women's Olympic hockey team.

After her grade-nine year, Saulnier was faced with two roads. On one path, she could stay in the only home she'd ever known in Nova Scotia, but scouts with Hockey Canada might never find her there. The other path, the one she chose, was a fourteen-hour drive away from home at a prep school in Massachusetts. Christine Brennan still remembers watching her daughter wander into the dining hall in an oversized green-and-white jersey. "She was only fifteen years old, and we're just driving away in silence," she recalled. Saulnier's parents didn't speak in the car for at least an hour on the way back. They felt numb.

Saulnier was desperately homesick. Her parents got her a cell phone so she could keep in touch, and the long distance bill was exorbitant in those first few months. As hard as it was, this marked the beginning of a journey that took Saulnier from Massachusetts to elite girls' hockey in the Toronto area to the Ivy League's Cornell University, to the national team and all the way to the Olympics in 2018. Saulnier faced ups and downs and sacrifices beyond moving away from home at fifteen. She used to keep mandatory daily logs of her life, from what she ate to how she felt, all to be sent off in the mail to Hockey Canada on a strict deadline. Brennan remembers telling her daughter she didn't have to do it anymore if she got tired of it. But Saulnier didn't want to quit.

Saulnier left home years ago, but she'll always be a Maritimer. With that comes pride. In an often-overlooked part of the country, one person's achievement belongs to everyone. It wasn't until she came back home and started seeing how people reacted to the silver medal that Saulnier began to feel proud of the second-place finish. "You never dream as a hockey player to go to the Olympics and win a silver medal," she said in an interview in 2022. "That's not the face that I ever expected to see in the mirror. To see the happiness and the excitement of others when they got to wear it was pretty cool, and I think that's when my sights and my view on it kind of turned." She realized that her biggest disappointment could bring a lot of joy to a place that had done a lot for her, and she made a promise to herself to get that medal into as many hands as possible. She wanted people to try on the medal, to bite it if they wanted. She felt it belonged to them just as much as it did to her.

One night, at an event at the casino in Halifax, one woman was too shy to put the medal on. Saulnier urged her to wear it, telling her it would look better on her. A photographer captured what happened next, frame by frame, when the medal fell, rolled around on the floor of the casino, and broke. The woman felt awful, but Saulnier didn't. She was just happy the medal had brought so much joy to people in a place she loves. That's at the heart of what she's done in this province since then, whether it's organizing a charity hockey game for a family who lost seven children in a house fire in 2019 or, after finally getting that Olympic gold medal she dreamed about in 2022, starting a foundation to benefit various causes around the province.

Winning gold gave Saulnier a confidence her mother hadn't seen in her before. It stood out to Christine Brennan when she watched her daughter give a Chamber of Commerce speech in Antigonish, Nova Scotia, a few months after winning gold. Saulnier talked about her role on the team: to lift up her teammates. "It's like anything else can happen now," Brennan said. "She's good. She's golden. She doesn't have to stress about anything. She has it." But a few months later, when the PWHPA tour visited her home province in November 2022, Saulnier was chasing one goal: to create the league the players had been working toward since 2019.

Even though Saulnier was an Olympic gold medallist, reaching the highest pinnacle in her sport, it didn't mean she was set for life. Saulnier won gold on the national team's fourth line. She wasn't Poulin, the player people looked to in overtime. Her role was more about supporting her teammates in whatever way they needed her or giving her team some extra energy on the ice. It's a role that doesn't always come with job security. A few months after winning gold, she didn't make Team Canada's world championship team. She found herself juggling hockey with a new career in real estate and taking a program at Harvard on the side, trying to find different ways to make a living. "We get up in the morning. We train," Saulnier said during the PWHPA's Nova Scotia showcase. "We try to be the best in the world at hockey, but we also have to be the best in the world to make money and to be able to live as well. It's a lot of balls in the air. But the best people in the world can juggle."

Such is life as a female pro hockey player.

While Turnbull, Saulnier, and the rest of the players worked on the ice in the fall of 2022, the PWHPA's goal was moving forward, slowly, behind the scenes.

For a long time, many people—including the PWHPA—thought the way forward was for the NHL to fund a new women's hockey league. In 2021, Sportsnet's Jeff Marek reported that the NHL told both the PWHPA and the existing American league (the NWHL) that it wouldn't fund a new league while there was already one in place—especially as the NHL recovered from the COVID-19 pandemic. A merger between the two sides hadn't come together over two years, either. At the beginning, many thought the PWHPA would be short lived, that someone would step in to figure something out right away. When that didn't happen, the PWHPA's leadership decided to stop waiting. They'd do the work themselves. In 2021, the PWHPA hired consultants from Deloitte to write a business plan, including financial models and research on potential markets. That research created the structure of the league they envisioned and was key information that would be useful to potential investors.

By the time the 2022–23 tour began in the fall of 2022, the PWHPA leadership felt they'd found the right investor. A few months earlier, as *The Athletic*'s Hailey Salvian first reported, they'd signed a letter of intent to work with Billie Jean King Enterprises and the Mark Walter Group to create a new professional women's hockey league. Walter is the chairman and controlling owner of the Los Angeles Dodgers baseball team and the CEO of the investment firm Guggenheim Partners. Forbes puts his net worth at about $6 billion. Jayna Hefford said the PWHPA felt the Walter Group would be a good fit. Not only did it have the money needed to bankroll something as massive as a professional sports league, but the PWHPA knew their values aligned with those of Walter and his wife, Kimbra, thanks to their relationship with Billie Jean King and Ilana Kloss. King and Kloss have been members of the Dodgers ownership group since 2018 and played a big role in convincing the Walters to invest in a women's hockey league. "I think that's one of the things we learned along the way," Hefford said in an interview a few years later. "You really have to make sure your values are aligned with the people you're going to work with."

The PWHPA handed over its business plan, and it was up to the investors to decide if they wanted to move forward. There was still no guarantee it would happen. To try to move things forward, Walter brought in a guy he knew could get things done: Stan Kasten.

On November 20, 2022, Kasten met Walter in his Santa Monica office, overlooking the beach and the iconic Ocean Avenue. It was the night of Elton John's final concert at Dodger Stadium. But before they could go to the show, they had a lot of business to go over. While they were chatting, Walter brought up the idea of creating a women's hockey league, a topic Kasten hadn't expected. Walter was frustrated the idea hadn't moved forward, and he asked Kasten to get it done.

Born in New Jersey, Kasten is a straight shooter who says it like he sees it. But he also isn't in the business of saying no to Walter. So when Walter asked him to take over the women's hockey league project, Kasten said yes, without really knowing exactly where it was going to lead him or what he'd just agreed to take on.

Kasten has a reputation for making things happen. He was only twenty-seven when he was hired to run the NBA's Atlanta Hawks as general manager in 1979, turning that team into a contender and winning NBA Executive of the Year awards in back-to-back seasons. The run of success continued in baseball when he led the Atlanta Braves to more wins than any other MLB team. The team won fourteen straight division titles and the World Series in 1995. After a stint with the Washington Nationals, Kasten joined Walter as part of the group that bought the Dodgers. He became team president when the sale closed.

Kasten is also used to juggling different balls at once. In 1999, when the NHL awarded Atlanta an expansion franchise that became the Thrashers, Kasten was president of three different pro sports teams in three different leagues at the same time. He had experience building from the ground up. But women's hockey was brand new to him. Walter wasn't happy with the preliminary work that had been done, so Kasten's first step was to stop everything and give himself thirty days to learn what this whole thing was all about. To make sure it was done right, Kasten decided he'd have to start from scratch.

While he was doing his homework, Kasten started meeting with some of the owners in the NWHL, which had since rebranded as the Premier Hockey Federation (PHF), to learn more about the landscape of professional women's hockey. Kasten asked Royce Cohen to sit in with him on some of those early meetings. He knew they'd be talking about a lot of finance issues, which were Cohen's specialty. Cohen rose through the Dodgers organization by using data to transform the way the team sold tickets, ultimately becoming the Dodgers' senior vice-president of business strategy. Hockey was new to Cohen, too, but he latched onto the project immediately. Kasten would later describe him as one of the most important people in making the new league happen. Both did the work on top of their day jobs with the Dodgers.

Kasten didn't know where the discussions with the PHF would lead and whether there would be some way for the entities to come together. He knew how much King and Kloss meant to the Walters and how important a women's hockey league was to them. Kasten would later describe King as the "spiritual leader" of the project. He knew that Walter didn't want it to fail and was counting on Kasten to push things over the finish line.

5
A LEAGUE IS BORN

March 2023
Toronto, Ontario

A few weeks before they became the last team to lift the PHF's Isobel Cup championship trophy, Toronto Six players were practising inside Canlan Ice Sports, a rink on the York University campus. Inside the facility, players had their own dressing room, prime ice time, and access to a weight room, things that hadn't always been standard within professional women's hockey. Playoffs were set to begin in a few days. A championship game was scheduled for later that month, but on this day, the players still didn't know where in North America it was going to be played.

The Six was founded in 2020, giving the PHF (formerly the American NWHL) a footprint in Canada after the CWHL folded in 2019. But many of the top Canadian players refused to play in the PHF, including nearly all of the national-team stars. Instead, they were members of the Professional Women's Hockey Players Association (PWHPA) and travelled around North America on the Dream Gap Tour, with the goal of starting a new league that would feel more professional to them. Not having those stars in the fold didn't stop the PHF from continuing to grow and, in many ways, develop more professional working conditions in the process. The league added another

Canadian team in 2022–23 in Montréal, and with COVID-19 restrictions a thing of the past, that season felt more normal for the league.

Hockey Hall of Famer Angela James had become general manager of the Six a year earlier, and the previous fall, the team had hired retired goaltender Sami Jo Small, one of the founders of the CWHL, as team president. Earlier that winter, the team had made headlines when it lured former top NCAA player Daryl Watts out of an early retirement to join the Six. Her contract would pay her $150,000 the next season, making her the highest-paid female hockey player ever. That came after the PHF announced it would increase its salary cap to $1.5 million the next season. This prompted some PWHPA players to move over to play in the PHF. Leading scorer Loren Gabel was one of the most notable to make the switch in the 2022–23 season, but the salary promises had yet to shake the solidarity of the Canadian and American national-team groups.

Years of competing entities—first the CWHL and the NWHL, and later the NWHL/PHF and the PWHPA—created a narrative in the media of a "rift" in women's hockey. A significant amount of the coverage about women's professional hockey, especially in big outlets, focused on the division between PWHPA and PHF. Many felt things couldn't move forward until there was only one league with all the best players and no divide. Months after the CWHL folded, American star Hilary Knight compared the PHF to "a glorified beer league," drawing ire among PHF fans. When she had played in the league (then still called the NWHL), she'd called for more transparency on the source of the league's money after the league announced it would have to slash players' salaries in the middle of a season. But the two sides pushed each other forward at different times: first the NWHL/PHF by paying players for the first time and then the PWHPA by standing up and speaking out about what a true professional league should look like.

A 2021 *Sociology of Sport* research paper by academics Courtney Szto, Ann Pegoraro, Erin Morris, and Katrina Galas, co-authored with several others, including former players, framed the issue as two different approaches to feminism. The NWHL/PHF took the approach of staying the course and making incremental gains, while the PWHPA favoured big, radical change. The friction between the two sides, particularly after Knight's "beer league" comments, they argued, took attention away from the root issues that plagued women's hockey. "The work that takes place in maligning Knight's comments distracts us from the cause of her dissatisfaction, which is neither about the NWHL's infrastructure, or skill level, nor the closure of the CWHL," the paper's authors wrote. "The collective dissatisfaction stems from the sexism that women athletes face on a daily basis that has resulted in the options of playing for part-time wages or not playing at all."

It was that incremental-change approach that drew Johanna and John Boynton to the NWHL/PHF, where they ultimately held ownership in several teams in the league, including the Six. Johanna Boynton grew up outside Philadelphia, spending winter on a frozen pond with the boys and dads in her neighbourhood. Her parents snuck her onto ice hockey teams when she was young. She dressed at home so no one would be the wiser.

Women's hockey was just beginning to grow as Boynton went through high school, in part thanks to Title IX. Her high school started a girls' team about that time, and that led her to an opportunity to play collegiate hockey at Harvard University. After graduating, Boynton stayed involved in the sport however she could. In 2014, that meant billeting a number of players on the United States women's Olympic hockey team, helping players find housing while they trained, and raising money to take the players' families to Russia to watch the games. Those relationships convinced the Boyntons to get involved in the PHF when the league started pursuing independent ownership for its teams. Both Boyntons are entrepreneurs: Johanna is co-founder and CEO of a construction company, while John has also co-founded and invested in a number of businesses, including Russian tech companies.

The Boyntons felt the PWHPA players had valid reasons for not wanting to play in the league and believed they could address those issues from within. They hoped their familiarity with players in the 2014 Olympics could help win the trust of the PWHPA players, with the goal of working together.

The Boyntons and the other owners made a change at the top, hiring baseball executive Ty Tumminia to take over as PHF commissioner from Dani Rylan Kearney. They also revamped the governance structure of the league. Now a board of owners that met weekly would run things. They wrote league bylaws and a constitution. Their aim was to keep growing the league and players' salaries, though it wasn't enough to convince the PWHPA that the PHF was the sustainable league the players had long sought. Those players had sat out for several years and had a clear vision of what they wanted. Over the next couple of years, the PHF and the PWHPA spoke multiple times, but a merger never came to fruition. NHL commissioner Gary Bettman offered to mediate at one point, Boynton said, and even commissioned a consultant group to work with all sides to chart a vision. The final meeting between Bettman, the PHF, and the PWHPA happened in March 2022 at Bettman's office in New York. According to Boynton, the PHF wanted to work together, but the PWHPA ultimately voted to end talks of a merger for good.

"It disappointed me that it didn't gain traction," Boynton said in a 2024 interview. "Candidly, I think our owners and everybody were really counting on getting some [movement toward a merger]. But it didn't happen. The players had different people they were talking to."

That was Billie Jean King Enterprises and the Mark Walter Group, and by the end of 2022, Stan Kasten. When he took over, Stan began conversations with the PHF. By that point, USA Hockey executive Reagan Carey had succeeded Tumminia as commissioner of the PHF, and she handled many of those early meetings with Kasten. "The initial conversations were he was just doing his due diligence," Boynton said. "'What have you got here? What do you do? How does it work?' Really from square one. That took some time."

At first, it wasn't clear how those talks might end. Everyone kept them confidential—Boynton estimated only about six to eight people knew about the discussions and the nature of what they were talking about. The final road that process would lead them on would end up taking a lot longer to navigate than anyone imagined.

While talks continued between the PHF and the PWHPA, the players' association continued its tour across North America. At the end of February, the tour went to Wesley Chapel, Florida, to play three days of games in partnership with the NHL's Tampa Bay Lightning. The PWHPA set up shop in the AdventHealth Center Ice complex, a five-rink facility. Volunteers filled water bottles and stocked snacks for players, who shared the building with kids rollerblading to and from their ice times.

Just a few days earlier in Quebec, the Canadian national team had completed a reverse sweep against the Americans in the annual

Canada–United States Rivalry Series. During one of those games, Marie-Philip Poulin was honoured as the first woman to win the Northern Star Award as Canadian athlete of the year, plus the Bobbie Rosenfeld Award for the Canadian Press female athlete of the year. That same night, she registered her two hundredth point in a Canadian jersey.

It had been a busy season for the national-team players. But it had also been busy for the PWHPA players and staff who put on the showcases across North America while working full-time jobs outside of hockey. Take Team Adidas forward Kelly Gribbons, for example. On the first day of the Florida showcase, Gribbons scored the game-winning goal in a 3–2 victory against Team Sonnet with a little more than eight minutes left in the game. She played another two games over the next two days before flying back to Toronto late on Sunday night, and she was back at work as an electrical engineer on Monday morning. She also practised two nights a week and took classes for her MBA one night a week. And then she did it all again the weekend after the trip to Florida, when the PWHPA tour moved to Washington, DC. Her story wasn't unique. "It's definitely busy, but I like it, and a lot of the girls have full-time jobs that they go back to," Gribbons said in Florida.

Beyond the six games that weekend in Florida, there was chatter about the players forming a union. Publicly, they didn't yet have an employer, but for the last couple of months, they'd been negotiating a collective bargaining agreement with the investor group that would ultimately own their new league. Five members of the PWHPA board represented the players at the bargaining table: Brianne Jenner, Liz Knox, Hilary Knight, Kendall Coyne Schofield, and Sarah Nurse. Even though the league didn't exist yet, having a union from the beginning of the process was about protecting the players and making sure they would always have a voice, Nurse said that weekend in Florida. "That's the biggest thing because we need to be protected so that we can go out and be the best that we can possibly be," she said. "To have that from the outset is going to be very important and something that really hasn't been done before. It's exciting to think of the future."

On the other side was Stan Kasten. He kept hearing from the players that, above anything else, they wanted to be treated as professionals. "That's exactly what I wanted, what Mark wanted," Kasten recalled. "We actually knew what those conditions look like. We knew how to deliver it. But we can't do this unless it really shows signs that someday it is a business. It's not a charity. It's got to turn out to look like a business someday. They understood that."

At about the same time, Kasten met the PWHPA's operations consultant, Jayna Hefford, in person for the first time. As they sat face to face in his office in Los Angeles, she heard his excitement. "Stan's a pretty upfront guy. There's not much he holds back on," Hefford said. "It was just great to see that and that confidence in him in what he does and his beliefs. You don't have to guess what he's thinking. He'll tell you what he's thinking." Kasten developed an instant respect for Hefford. The two would work side by side on the day-to-day process of creating the new league, except when it came to collective bargaining. Both sides felt it would be best if Hefford sat that part out. That put Hefford in the position of knowing things were happening but having them be largely out of her hands. Kasten was under a non-disclosure agreement in the discussions with the PHF, and collective bargaining was confidential, too. All she could do was wait and keep running the Dream Gap Tour.

A few weeks later, in March 2023, the players gathered in California for their championship weekend. On the ice, Team Harvey's, which had dominated all season long, defeated Team Scotiabank 5–4 to win the championship game, powered by four points each from Jessie Eldridge and Emily Clark. The team cleaned up at the PWHPA's awards ceremony, too, where the association handed out prizes to players voted on by their peers. Poulin, defender Lee Stecklein, and goaltender Ann-Renée Desbiens won the top awards for their positions, while their coach, Kori Cheverie, took home the award for the best coach.

Off the ice that weekend, the players got a small taste of what was happening behind the scenes. The media had been speculating about what the future league could look like and when it might be announced. The larger player group didn't know full details yet, either. The players met in two groups at the Margaritaville Resort in Palm Springs, California, with Kasten. This was the first time they could put a face to the rumblings they'd been hearing about what the PWHPA's league could look like and who would pay for it. It was also the first time Kasten met players other than the leaders he'd spent hours with in video calls during collective bargaining negotiations. Kasten warned the players that, should things move forward, they were going to screw up in the first year. "We'll fix it in year two and after. Don't worry about it," Kasten told them. "We're doing this together; we're experimenting together."

The message was one of confidence, but even in March 2023, nearly four years after the players had decided to sit out, it still wasn't a guarantee that the league would come to fruition. Still, what Kasten saw that weekend gave him comfort. True, the PWHPA had a hard time filling the stands for its championship game, but they hadn't had much time to promote it. "I still saw that what they were doing among themselves was extraordinarily professional looking, other than the attendance," Kasten recalled. "They'd been doing this on their own, and that was very impressive to me because I know how hard that is, and I know how many things are involved in that. To have sponsors and equipment and merchandise and stuff like that was very impressive. That put the idea into my head, which may be the single best idea I had: I don't need to look anywhere for the hockey side." Kasten hadn't hired anyone else to work in the league because it wasn't a certainty yet that there would be a league. The work so far had been done mostly by just Kasten and Royce Cohen and whomever they needed to call upon down the hall of the Dodgers office to help with this or that. But Kasten knew that when the day came, Hefford would lead hockey operations.

After months of collective bargaining and negotiations with the PHF, both pieces of the puzzle came together around the same time, entirely by chance. "We came to the conclusion that it would make more sense for us to buy the other league, shut them down as they were, and instead use the assets we were acquiring to put them into what we thought would be just a different, upscale version of what they'd been trying to do," explained Stan Kasten, who led those negotiations on behalf of the investor group. "That made a lot of sense to me."

After six months of negotiating, a tentative collective bargaining agreement was in place with the players, too. Before moving forward, however, Kasten needed a final decision from Mark Walter. Back he went to the Santa Monica office overlooking the beach, where Kasten and Royce Cohen explained to Walter what both deals might look like. They didn't sugarcoat that it would be expensive, though the ownership group has never revealed just how much money they put in.

"So you're telling me at the end of ten years, it's going to cost me this much money?" Kasten remembers Walter asking.

"Yep," Kasten replied.

"We're going to own the whole league?"

"Yep."

"We're going to own all the teams?

"Yep."

"And we're going to do something good?"

"Yeah."

The ownership group has a stake in other women's sport properties, including the WNBA's Los Angeles Sparks. Ultimately, according to Kasten, the idea of creating something different from the ground up for female athletes appealed to the Walters, and they gave the green light. "This version of what we did never existed before," Kasten said in an interview a little more than a year later. "Not with full front offices, and full media, and real venues with real practice facilities, and real training, staff and equipment, and meals and housing allowances and maternity leave." Many of those things were enshrined in the collective bargaining agreement, the first time a brand-new league had something like that in place from day one.

The eight-year deal spelled out that players in the new league would make $55,000 on average in the first season, with a 3 per cent salary increase each season. No one would earn less than $35,000, but that doesn't go far in a major city. The players signed to one-year deals would have less job security in their contracts, with teams having the right to terminate those deals. But it also included language about maternity leave, hours of work, and when teams would provide meals, typical benefits for professional athletes but not always part of professional female hockey players' worlds. They were game changers. The agreement also included a housing stipend of $1,500 per month for contracted players, a figure that would increase in each subsequent season, and help with finding housing.

On June 26, 2023, after Kasten got the green light from Walter, he called Jayna Hefford to tell her it was done. Much like the players, she had blind trust and was patiently waiting to find out what would happen. Until that phone call came, she wasn't certain it would. "We all knew it was real at that point," Hefford recalled. Players in the PWHPA ratified the collective bargaining agreement with the league a few days later, on July 2.

Meanwhile, while negotiations were ongoing with the new league's investors, the PHF had been signing players to contracts all summer. The negotiation conversations were confidential, and the only way to make sure word didn't leak out was to operate as business as usual, even though the owners knew things could dramatically change depending on the outcome of the negotiations. If they fell through, the PHF needed teams and players in place for the next season, which would go ahead as planned. This meant players were signing contracts with no idea that, ultimately, the league they had just signed to play in might no longer exist. Reflecting back on those circumstances more than a year later, Johanna Boynton still found it painful. "You hope that the lasting effect isn't that they think you're an untrustworthy dirt ball," she said. "I still struggle to envision how we would have done it differently, to work with something where we didn't really have a whole lot of control over it but had to be strictly confidential. That was really hard."

The negotiations also took longer than everyone expected, and in the end, things looked a bit different than the Boyntons had envisioned. They'd been hoping more staff from the PHF would find work in the PWHL, for example. Only a couple of people did, as the new league hired from scratch. But the goal had been to unify women's hockey, and that goal was accomplished. When things were finalized, PHF players were invited to a call where they learned their league had been sold and would shut down. This marked a seismic shift in the pro women's hockey landscape, one many didn't see coming. The players, staff, and fans who loved the PHF and its teams were heartbroken to see the whole thing disappear overnight. It was the same kind of pain the CWHL fans had experienced a few years earlier, knowing they'd never get to watch their favourite teams play again.

PHF players had made life plans based on the contracts they'd signed in the league. Now, those deals were void, though severance was available for players who watched their contracts disappear. With only six pro hockey teams in North America the next season instead of eleven, some PHF and PWHPA players weren't going to have a roster spot. Some retired and found jobs outside of hockey. Some moved on to European teams. Others made a team in the new league but played a different role on the ice than they had in the PHF. Some who had been on the first line on their old team would play lower in the lineup in the new league. But the majority of players also acknowledged that having a single league was best for the game, and that women's hockey had needed it for years. Player leaders within the PHF issued a statement a few days after news of the sale broke. "We look to depart from the divisive narrative that too often plagued the many great achievements across professional women's hockey, and become unified as we collectively create hockey's future," it read. "As we embark on another league formation, we bring the power and the infrastructure we fought to build. We are hugely excited to see a unified league that will house all of the best athletes that hockey has to offer and aim to build the strongest league that can stand the test of time."

After calling Hefford, Kasten's second phone call was to NHL commissioner Gary Bettman. Kasten hadn't spoken to Bettman about the project during the seven months since Walter asked him to take the lead on it. He hadn't wanted to be another person who had big plans for women's hockey but didn't follow through. He only made the call when he could say it was done. Bettman, Kasten said, thought the news was fantastic. The NHL wouldn't provide financial assistance to the league, but it did begin to offer help with things like scheduling, officiating, and hosting games in NHL venues.

There was a lot to be done and no staff yet, beyond Hefford, Kasten, and Cohen, to do it. They needed to finalize the name of the league, lock down exact markets for teams, figure out where those teams would be playing, how players would be distributed to those teams, create a schedule...and the list went on. It would all have to be done by January 1, 2024, the league's scheduled start date. Hefford had convinced Kasten that the league needed to begin play that season. The players could not miss any more time than they already had. Come January, some wouldn't have played a competitive game in nine months, and many of the PWHPA players hadn't played in a league for four and a half years. Hefford warned him that the players might not stay with the league if they missed a full season. Some would move on with their lives and other jobs. "I wish I had known how difficult that would be, because then I wouldn't have done it," Kasten said of the January 1 start date. "It was stupid to try. But because we had drawn a line in the sand, we had no choice. We gotta make it happen."

Hefford started driving around to different markets to look at arenas. She also started building a hockey operations staff and planning what the league's first draft could look like, feeling like that was the best way to create parity and make the league competitive. They also had to hire general managers for each of the six teams, so they could start building their rosters. A staffer with the Dodgers drew up a tentative schedule for the six teams, which they had to throw out when the ownership group chose different markets in July. They settled on having teams in Toronto, Montréal, Ottawa, Boston, Minnesota, and the New York area. Ottawa was a bit of a surprise and hadn't been part of the original plan. There hadn't been a professional women's hockey team in Ottawa since 2010, when the Ottawa CWHL team folded. Without the ability to pay salaries, that team had struggled to attract national-team players away from hubs in Toronto and Montréal. Bettman, though, told Kasten not to discount Ottawa as a market, and that went a long way to making it one of the final cities. Once those six cities were set in stone, things started to feel more real.

Kasten and Hefford had been part of a lot of press conferences over their years in sports, but this was the first time either of them had launched a brand-new league in an online video meeting. It was August 29, 2023, and nearly two months after the PHF acquisition. While Kasten and Hefford, who was named the new league's senior vice-president of hockey operations, were busy behind the scenes putting the pieces together for the first season, players and fans wondered when they'd finally know more about the league, including, most importantly, when they would play again. All they could do was wait.

The night before that first press conference, about three hundred of the best players from across the world had been invited to a call so they could get information about the new league before details became public. Some of the answers came in that call. The next day, the public learned the new league would be called the Professional Women's Hockey League and discovered where the six teams would be based. The teams would begin play in January 2024 and play twenty-four games each in that first season. In the future, the schedule would be bigger, and the season would start earlier; for now, they just wanted to get on the ice. No schedule was available yet, nor did the teams have names or logos. The teams also didn't have confirmed home venues yet, and it was late in the year to be looking for arena availability,

Kasten admitted. "Putting all of those things together and working around the problem of building availabilities in every city has been complex," Kasten said that day. "It's going to continue to be complex, and that's going to take us a little time."

On the hockey side, Hefford described how she'd pulled together a player evaluation committee that made a list of a wide pool of players who could compete in the league. They wanted to attract not just the best of the best coming out of the university and college ranks and the top players who had already played in the PHF or PWHPA, but also draw the best players internationally. The PHF led the way in that regard: the season before, players from ten different countries had competed. But traditionally, the lack of a livable wage prevented some of the best talent from outside North America from making the move.

Teams would have a short window to sign three foundational players each ahead of the draft, which was set to be held in Toronto in less than three weeks. Beyond those eighteen players, the rest of the player pool had to wait and see where they'd be drafted, and if their name wasn't called, try to secure a free-agent training camp invitation. Players had to self-register for the draft, with the league vetting who was eligible based on what level of hockey they had played. For many players who entered the draft, it was the first time they had no control over where they'd be playing and living. "This draft is a really exciting moment for all of women's hockey," Hefford said at the first league press conference. "It's never been done in a way that GMs and teams select players they think can help them win a championship, that hasn't been based on convenience for players, and we've talked about that a lot. There's going to be a strong level of integrity to this draft. You're going to a team that wants you and thinks you can compete, not because you happen to have a home or family in the market. The integrity is incredibly important to the players."

The press conference also served to introduce the recently hired executive director of the Professional Women's Hockey League Players Association, the players' union: veteran hockey executive Brian Burke, who'd spent time working in the NHL head office and with several different teams. Women's hockey wasn't new to him. He'd been a fan since it made its debut at the 1998 Olympics and was a big supporter of the CWHL, even serving on the league's board. When he worked for the Calgary Flames, Burke spent a lot of time around the CWHL's Calgary Inferno team. He watched those players share a roll of tape and borrow laces from one another. "I have seen the hardships they've gone through, the iterations they've gone through to get there to play and put this together," Burke said at the press conference. "I'm so proud to be involved, so it was a very emotional moment for me when they offered me the job."

With six city names and not much else, it was hard to imagine exactly how these teams might look. So much was left to be done to build the teams from scratch. In addition to venues, a schedule, and player distribution, the league still needed a rulebook, medical standards, and broadcast deals, the kind of stuff already in place in a league like the NHL that's been around for more than one hundred years. Staff needed to be hired at the league level, and teams needed staff and equipment, too. The teams didn't even have things like skate-sharpening machines. Within a couple of months, teams would need to hold training camps to prepare for the season. A January launch seemed increasingly ambitious.

6
FROM THE GROUND UP

September 2023
Montréal, Quebec

It was no surprise to anyone in Quebec that Danièle Sauvageau was the woman chosen to build the PWHL Montréal team from scratch as its general manager. Sauvageau is a giant in women's hockey in her province and across the country, a woman who is synonymous with the sport. She's also a builder by nature, whether it's building a high-performance centre for the best female hockey players in Quebec or, in this case, building a whole franchise from the ground up. Becoming general manager of a professional women's hockey team was a job Sauvageau only could have dreamed about when she discovered the game as a child. "This position is a pinnacle, [after] growing the game over the last few years," Sauvageau said on September 1, 2023, when she and the other five general managers were introduced to the media on an online video call.

Had it not been for Sauvageau's persistence and drive, and her deep desire to be a part of the game she loves, there might have been no hockey career at all.

Sauvageau will never forget the day she went to the rink in Saint-Eustache, a Montréal suburb, to sign up to play hockey. She was twelve years old and had spent years playing on an outdoor rink with her brothers in Deux-Montagnes, a suburb northwest of Montréal.

Sauvageau's parents wanted their kids to grow up near a park; that's why they chose their home on Thirteenth Avenue in Deux-Montagnes, where they moved when Sauvageau was four. In the winter, the kids were always on the rink, and in the summer, they were swimming at the community pool and playing baseball.

But when it came time to register to play organized hockey, only Sauvageau's brothers were allowed to sign up. Almost fifty years later, she still remembers the eyes of the man who said no—and the hurt she felt at the rejection. It was the first time she was told she couldn't do something because of her gender. Then Sauvageau asked a question that would change the rest of her life: "How can I help?" Even though she wouldn't be allowed to play, Sauvageau wanted to be involved in hockey in some way. She found herself on the bench, opening the door for players or filling up their water bottles. Sometimes, she could bring her skates and move pucks around during practice. It was a way to be around a sport that made her happy and a way for her to make things better. It took her years to figure out why she'd asked that question instead of walking away from the rink disappointed. She traced the answer back to her mother, whose involvement in their community she watched growing up and who instilled those values in her children.

Sauvageau started coaching boys' hockey and then women in the Ligue régionale de hockey au féminin. Her career took her to the first Winter Olympics featuring women's hockey in 1998, serving as an assistant coach. Canada had been dominant on the international stage since winning the first Women's World Championship in 1990. When the Canadians lost that first Olympic gold-medal game to the Americans, it was a wake-up call, proof that the rest of the world was starting to catch up. In 2002, in Salt Lake City, Sauvageau was the head coach when the Canadian women won an Olympic gold medal for the first time. She remembers the final seconds ticking down and feeling like they lasted forever. When the buzzer finally sounded, Sauvageau fell off the bench and cracked her rib. She didn't feel the pain for two days.

Sauvageau also coached young men in the Quebec Major Junior Hockey League, the first and only woman to ever do that. She did it all while working full time as a police officer. She saved up her overtime and took unpaid leave to travel to coach hockey. Sauvageau never wanted to become a police officer, but coaching women's hockey certainly didn't pay, and she needed a job.

She'd graduated from school as a social worker when she saw the ad for the Royal Canadian Mounted Police. She felt the job would blend law and social work, so she filled out an application. Her parents found out she'd applied to become a police officer when two men came to the door as part of the background check. She remembers her father's blue eyes staring at her that day as he asked her if that's what she really wanted to do. "I don't know," she said. "I'll find out."

Her career lasted more than three decades with the RCMP and Montréal's police service. Over that time, she worked on major crimes like the Dawson College school shooting and spent time in specialized units for drug crime and sexual violence. Hockey was always a love, though, and Sauvageau found herself drawn to jobs where she could give players the tools to be at their best, whether it was starting the women's hockey program at the University of Montréal or creating Centre 21.02 inside the Verdun Auditorium in 2019.

Sauvageau's hiring was the first step in building the PWHL Montréal team, and she had her work cut out for her to create a roster and hire staff quickly. A few days after her hiring was announced, Sauvageau could start signing the team's three foundational free agents to three-year contracts. There was no doubt Marie-Philip Poulin would be one of them. It was hard to imagine a team in

Montréal without the face of women's hockey in that province leading the way. Ann-Renée Desbiens seemed certain, too. After leaving the 2018 Olympics with a silver medal, Desbiens had stepped away from the sport. An accountant by trade, she saw a brighter future there than in hockey. But she couldn't stay away for long, and it was Desbiens who starred for Canada in net during a dominant 2022 Olympic gold-medal win. She was from Quebec and also happened to be one of the best goaltenders in the world.

To local fans, Laura Stacey may have been the least known of Montréal's first three signings. The forward from Kleinburg, Ontario, won an Olympic gold medal alongside Poulin and Desbiens in 2022 but did so further down the lineup. Some may have known her only because she and Poulin had announced their engagement a few months earlier. But her connection to Poulin wasn't why Sauvageau signed her. Stacey had been one of the best players in the PWHPA circuit the season before. A strong power forward standing five-foot-ten, Stacey has a drive to the net that rivals anyone in women's hockey. She'd used her speed and size to put up twenty-one points in twenty games with Team Adidas the season before and tie for fourth in the PWHPA in scoring. She's one of the fastest players in women's hockey, and her size would become an asset in a league that would be more physical than many could have imagined. Those people who questioned the signing also may not have known about the leadership Stacey brings off the ice and what it's like to be her teammate. At some of PWHL Montréal's hardest moments in the first season, Stacey was one of the players fielding tough questions from reporters. On the day the three free agents were unveiled, Stacey told reporters in French that she was proud to play in the city. She grew up in Ontario cheering for the Toronto Maple Leafs, but Montréal had been her home for the last few years. "It's something we all dreamed about as little kids. Seeing it happen today, it's hard to put it into words, but I think sitting here beside Danièle, Ann, and Marie-Philip today, it leaves us speechless." The three described the culture they wanted to build in Montréal: a lot of heart, hard work, and fun. "We really value good people and good ambassadors," Desbiens told reporters. "Yes, obviously there's going to be a lot of talented hockey players, a lot of skills on the ice. But we also want good people in the dressing room, good teammates. That's what we think is very important."

They were PWHL Montréal's foundation, and within a couple weeks, they would be at the draft in Toronto, watching several new teammates be selected. But first, Sauvageau had to publicly name the coach who'd be sitting with her at the draft table. That was Kori Cheverie, a thirty-six-year-old rising star Sauvageau had worked with on Team Harvey's in the PWHPA the previous season, winning the PWHPA championship together. Sauvageau came away from working with Cheverie impressed not just with her hockey brain but also her ability to solve problems—a quality she learned at a young age.

Cheverie spent her early years living in Moosonee, a Cree community in remote northern Ontario. The youngest of three children, she was always competitive. Basketball and baseball came first, and Cheverie believed she would be the first female Toronto Blue Jay. Hockey started to intrigue her when she watched the Mighty Ducks movies in the 1990s. She still loves and references those movies today. When she was eight, her mother moved their family back east to her hometown of New Glasgow in Nova Scotia's Pictou County. There, all of Cheverie's friends were playing hockey, and they would come to school on Monday talking about their games over the weekend. She played road hockey every single day with her best friend, often waking up early to play before school. They'd pretend they were at tryouts for elite teams, wowing the coaches with their skills.

At about that time, Cheverie decided she wanted to play organized hockey like her friends. But money was tight. Cheverie's mother was raising the three children on her own. She was a teacher, but teaching jobs were hard to come by at that time. When they moved to Nova Scotia, she decided to start her own preschool. "Needing to or wanting to play sports was certainly something that wasn't just kind of taken for granted in our household," Cheverie recalled in an interview. "If you were going to play sports, you really had to kind of help with it." Despite the barrier, Cheverie was determined to play. After a couple of years of negotiations, ten-year-old Cheverie struck a deal with her mother: if she could come up with the money to buy her equipment, her mom would pay for her registration. Cheverie held a yard sale and made enough to buy a used bag of gear, and her mother held up her end of the deal.

Growing up watching her mother work so hard gave Cheverie a sense of work ethic and the determination to always find a way. She never takes anything for granted, not playing hockey or any of the opportunities that have come her way through the game. Even though she didn't play organized hockey until she was ten years old, the sport took her to the Canada Games, where she represented Nova Scotia. Then it took her to Saint Mary's University, where Cheverie captained the Huskies to an Atlantic University Sport championship in 2010. She knew she wanted to play professionally, after getting her mom to wake her up at the crack of dawn so she could watch games in the old National Women's Hockey League (those games never got prime-time billing). After she graduated, Cheverie entered the CWHL draft. Meanwhile, she moved across the country to play for a team in the Western Women's Hockey League (WWHL). When the Toronto Furies picked her in the draft, she headed back east again.

Over her six seasons with Toronto, the forward never missed a single game. Cheverie only ever missed one practice with an illness, maybe one she'd picked up in her day job working at a daycare in those early seasons. She won a Clarkson Cup championship with the Furies in 2014. But playing professionally didn't pay, and, like many women who weren't on the national team, she was mostly playing for fun by the end of her career. Cheverie was running some programs at Ryerson University (now Toronto Metropolitan University) when, in 2016, an assistant coaching job with the men's hockey team opened. She applied, got the job, and retired from playing hockey at twenty-nine to become the first woman to coach in a Canadian university men's program.

Most coaches can walk into a room and immediately feel that they command respect. Being a woman walking into a men's dressing room, when many of those men have never had a female coach before, requires some relationship building. That's exactly what Cheverie did, and her first coaching experience taught her to be prepared to handle any kind of situation. When, in 2022, a positive COVID test kept her from travelling with Team Canada to the Olympics, she found a way to be an assistant coach from home in Nova Scotia, relying on attention to detail to pick out key things in players' performances from afar. She changed her sleep schedule so she'd be aligned with her players in China. "I always say if you're going to hire a female coach, you're not going to regret it because you're going to get a really hard worker who's very prepared for every situation," she said. "Sometimes that comes from a place of feeling insecure or having that imposter syndrome, which obviously is not the greatest, and everyone works through that."

Cheverie's success led to her becoming the first woman to serve on the coaching staff of a men's national team at the 2022 Men's Under-18 World Championship. As an assistant coach with the women's national team, her resumé includes three world championships and an Olympic gold medal in 2022, when she supported the team remotely. Poulin, Desbiens, and Stacey were all on that team. It also led to opportunities coaching at development and training camps with NHL teams, including a stint with the Pittsburgh Penguins as a guest coach in 2023, where she stepped behind the bench to coach in the pre-season, one of the first two women to ever do that (the other, Jessica Campbell, was hired as an assistant coach with the NHL's Seattle Kraken in 2024).

All of that, from the hard work she had to do just to play the game she loved, to the determination it took to keep climbing the coaching ladder and making sure she was extra-prepared for anything thrown her way, led her to the next challenge at the end of summer 2023: head coach of a professional women's hockey team. Saying yes to the job was easy. During her own playing career, Montréal was always a special place to play. The fans cared so much about their team, and reporters were always invested in how the team was performing. She saw it as a once-in-a-lifetime opportunity that, like everything else in her life, she didn't take for granted. Her attention to detail and work ethic earned her a head coaching job, but so had her ability to connect with and care for her players as humans first, something she would bring with her to Montréal.

Working with Sauvageau was also special. Cheverie still has the poster of the 2002 gold-medal-winning Canadian women's Olympic team on her wall in Nova Scotia, with Sauvageau in the middle of the ice, her arms in the air and her fists clenched in celebration. She was the first woman Cheverie saw behind the bench. Now, they would work together to build PWHL Montréal—two women whose love for the game and determination got them where they are, despite all odds. At the heart of that relationship was an ability to be honest with each other, something that would come in handy with so many roster decisions awaiting the GM and coach.

On the day her hiring was announced, Sauvageau said she had no doubt Cheverie would be coaching somewhere in the league had Montréal not hired her. "We are very fortunate to have her here in Montréal," the GM said. Cheverie told the group she'd gotten to see what Sauvageau had built with Centre 21.02 firsthand, having worked with her on Team Harvey's in the PWHPA. What she built at the centre was something other regions could look to and try to replicate. "Danièle has a vision that I agree with," the coach said. "Our values align. It made complete sense. It was an easy transition to say yes to coming to Montréal and be a part of something really special."

They also agreed on another thing: the objective was to win. Both are fiercely competitive people, and they weren't shy about saying they wanted people on their team who are hungry to win, too. It wasn't like the men's team in the city, where no one wanted to say the word *playoffs* quite yet. "You shouldn't be afraid to say you want to achieve the greatest title in the league and win the league," Cheverie said. "I think that's important and it's a common goal for a team to have. I'm not scared to speak in those terms."

"That's the objective, period," Sauvageau added.

Not long into the press conference, Cheverie was asked if she spoke French. "I knew this was coming," she said with a laugh. "No, but I am working on it." She knew how to ask to sharpen her pencil in French, but Cheverie admitted that phrase might not be that useful in hockey. Some French media criticized the decision to hire someone who only spoke English. It's not without precedent in Montréal. In 2011 the NHL team hired Randy Cunneyworth, a unilingual anglophone from Ontario, to great controversy. Cunneyworth wasn't able to speak to passionate Habs fans in their language. Cheverie's hiring raised the same questions among some reporters, even as Sauvageau assured them that her coach would learn the language.

Cheverie was taken aback by the reaction at the time, but she soon understood how important it is to be able to speak the language and how crucial that is to the culture of the province. It wasn't an empty promise. Cheverie meant it. She wanted to be able to communicate with fans, reporters, and players. She would have to show it, but Cheverie was determined to put as much hard work into learning French as she had with everything else in her career.

7
DRAFT DAY
September 18, 2023
Toronto, Ontario

For years, the best young male hockey players in the world have had the opportunity to hear their name called, walk on stage, and pull on an NHL team's sweater. The NHL draft has been held annually since 1963 and is part of every hockey-playing boy's hopes and dreams. Even though not all of the young men picked at each draft will play even a minute in the NHL, that day is still the realization of a dream. A team liked them enough to want them and give them an opportunity, and that's something few people get.

Historically, women haven't had the same moment to dream about. There were drafts in previous women's professional hockey leagues, but a lot of times, the players already knew where they'd be going. It wasn't fair to ask someone to move across the country to play for no money, so players were often selected by teams close to where they already lived or where they knew they could find other work.

There had never been a women's hockey draft quite like the one that took over the Barbara Frum Atrium at the CBC Broadcast Centre on September 18, 2023. Players got dressed up and walked down a purple carpet, where they posed for photos. Fans lined the carpet to get autographs. Seats were set aside for friends, family, and agents to cheer the players on. A media room of reporters waited to speak to every draft pick after their selection, and a CBC Sports panel analyzed the top picks for those watching the broadcast.

There were no sweaters for players to pull on that day. Teams didn't have names or logos yet, and the sweaters the players would wear in the first season, emblazoned with simply the city name, were still a couple of months away from being ready. Instead, players held up a wooden PWHL hockey stick with the city's name on it. But that didn't lessen the excitement that hung in the air all day long. It was all sponsored by Canadian Tire. A few days earlier, the league had announced it had signed a multi-year agreement for the company to become the PWHL's first major sponsor. It felt like a new beginning for the sport.

Just like in the NHL, each team's draft table buzzed in between picks as GMs went over their lists with their head coaches and a handful of staff members who'd recently been hired. Unlike the NHL, teams weren't allowed to trade draft picks in the first season, so wheeling and dealing would have to wait.

At the Montréal draft table sat general manager Danièle Sauvageau and head coach Kori Cheverie, who quickly perfected the art of discreet whispering as they avoided the prying eyes of the TV cameras. A couple of staff members, including director of analytics Mikael Nahabedian, sat at the table with them. An accountant by trade, Nahabedian made a name for himself by writing about advanced stats and women's hockey scouting online. He'd previously done analytics work for the PHF's Montréal Force, McGill University, and a club in Sweden. That he was sitting at the table that day said a lot about the value the organization placed on data and analytics.

A random draw weeks before had determined the draft order. Minnesota won the first pick, followed by Toronto, Boston, New York, Ottawa, and finally, Montréal. There were fifteen rounds in total, and the order reversed every second round, meaning Montréal also had the seventh-overall pick. TSN broadcaster Tessa Bonhomme took the stage to begin the draft. In 2010, Bonhomme had been the CWHL's first draft pick, so it felt appropriate for her to kick off this draft in a new era of women's hockey. She introduced advisory board member Billie Jean King, who made the trip to Toronto for a big moment in a league she'd believed in from the beginning. Her entrance drew a standing ovation from the crowd.

"Trailblazing is bold, it's brave, and it can be very scary and lonely," King told the crowd watching from the floor and on the CBC Sports broadcast. "But it's worth it. It's really worth it. It's worth it for each one of us who have fought so hard for this day, and it's worth it for the generations of girls and women who will come behind us." The new league, King said, would give professional female hockey players the structure, support, and platform they deserved. She acknowledged that they had a lot of work to do to earn fans' support. The league was just getting started. "Thank you to every woman who played this game who won't be lacing up her skates, but will be right there alongside us," King said. "To those who worked two jobs, bought her own equipment, who didn't [play] for glory or a paycheque, simply for the love of this magnificent game. To the leagues that came before and everyone who dreamed what today could look like. This is for all of us. And with that, I'm being told the first pick is in."

Without missing a beat, King announced the first player drafted into the PWHL. It was the name everyone expected her to say: twenty-three-year-old forward Taylor Heise. She was a rising star on Team USA, having been named MVP of the world championship a year earlier. Heise grew up in Lake City, Minnesota, played college hockey at the University of Minnesota, and would now be staying in her home state to play professionally. You couldn't have scripted it better.

Throughout the rest of the first round, defenders went off the board quickly. First, veteran defender Jocelyne Larocque was taken by Toronto, then Ella Shelton went to New York, and Savannah Harmon to Ottawa. In between, at third, Boston took Swiss superstar forward Alina Müller, who was only twenty-five but had been playing on her country's senior national team for a decade. At the end of the first round, Sauvageau took the stage to make her first pick. Montréal already had its starting goaltender, its first-line centre, and a top power forward signed for the next three years. Like many of the GMs who picked before her, Sauvageau needed a top defender. She selected Erin Ambrose, the national-team rearguard known for her strong hockey smarts and for always wearing her heart on her sleeve. Ambrose was very familiar with the three players already signed in Montréal. The twenty-nine-year-old grew up playing with Laura Stacey in Ontario, even living with her family for a bit in grade eleven. Marie-Philip Poulin had also become a close friend to Ambrose, and Ann-Renée Desbiens was no stranger, either. They'd all won a gold medal together on Team Canada the year before.

With the pick, Montréal added a player who could run the top power-play unit alongside Poulin and Stacey, and who thinks about the game in a way that few others do. Ask her about any game and Ambrose can explain what happened in a play, as if she has a hockey supercomputer living in her brain. The Montréal team also got a leader who had been through highs and lows in hockey and could bring some perspective to the team's younger players. Asked about the pick after the draft, Sauvageau pointed out the obvious: Ambrose is the one who can get the puck to Poulin. Who wouldn't want that?

Ambrose grinned as she walked to the stage, shook King's hand, and posed for a photo with King, Sauvageau, and Jayna Hefford.

Ambrose grew up playing with boys and watched some of them have their moment at the NHL draft. One of her friends had opted not to go to his draft in person, and Ambrose finally understood why he avoided the stress: she admitted to reporters afterward that she had dripped with sweat the entire time.

Ambrose's hair and makeup had been done earlier that day—elevated game-day attire, she called it. When she walked down the purple carpet, she spotted familiar logos on some of the kids' hockey jackets from teams she'd played for and against growing up. She couldn't help but reflect on how neat it was that they got to miss school to come to a women's hockey draft. But the best part was that Ambrose would be going back to Montréal. It felt full circle. The city had been a sanctuary for her six years earlier, a place that helped her deal with the heartbreak of not making the 2018 Olympic team. It was a turning point that changed her trajectory as a player and person.

Ambrose began struggling with her mental health as a teenager. She felt an emptiness that consumed her even as she reached new heights in her hockey career. She asked for help and began to address some of the root issues, starting with embracing her sexual orientation, a secret that had been weighing her down like a brick. It was then that she learned that other people in her family also struggled with their mental health and could help her through it. But that wasn't the end of it. In her first year at Clarkson University in 2012, Ambrose turned to hockey to mask an eating disorder. Even though she was at her lowest and found herself on academic probation, she was still succeeding on the ice, she explained in an article she wrote for Hockey Canada a few years later. Hockey could not always be her safe place, though, and when she couldn't use the sport to cover up what she was feeling inside, anxiety crept in. Routine helped with that anxiety; situations where she lacked control didn't.

Fast-forward to 2017, when Ambrose moved to Calgary for centralization, the months-long, gruelling process of trying out for the Canadian women's Olympic hockey team. Centralization was all consuming, requiring players to move their lives across the country in some cases and putting everything else aside in pursuit of one goal. Ambrose admitted in her article that she'd shown up at centralization out of shape but had to perform every day regardless of how her body or mind was feeling. She knew if she took a step back for one day, someone would be waiting to take her spot. When she was released from the team, her world collapsed beneath her. Everything in her life was built around being a hockey player, and she felt like she wasn't good enough at the one thing that had defined her. "This news crushed me," Ambrose wrote in her Hockey Canada article. "I didn't know how I could face my family. I felt like I had let them down. Within a day, I also lost the opportunity to be around my teammates and closest friends, and my ultimate goal of playing in the Olympics."

Players had access to complimentary flights during centralization year, and Stacey hadn't used hers. She let Ambrose use her credits to fly to Montréal after she was released. Ambrose went to visit goaltender Emerance Maschmeyer, whom she knew dating back to their time on Canada's under-18 team. Maschmeyer also hadn't made the Olympic team and understood what Ambrose was going through. The national team was on the road, so Ambrose wouldn't see anyone from the Hockey Canada program in Montréal. It was the escape from hockey Ambrose needed.

When her flight back to Calgary landed, Ambrose texted Team Canada's general manager at the time, Mel Davidson, and told her she wanted to discuss moving to Montréal. Part of it, Ambrose admitted years later, was running away. She didn't want to see people in Toronto who would constantly want to talk about her release from the team. In Montréal, Ambrose found community and eventually, she found her love for hockey again. In addition to Maschmeyer, to whom she gravitated like a light in the darkness that season, she found family in Caroline Ouellette and Julie Chu, hockey legends whom Ambrose had always admired as players. The couple run one of the best Canadian university women's hockey programs, at Concordia. Ambrose started coaching with them and found she loved being on the ice and working with the players. Chu and Ouellette became like second mothers to her.

Ambrose also found her way back as a player with Les Canadiennes in the CWHL. She looked at her time in Montréal as a chance to prove herself, what she described years later as a *fuck-you* mentality. It showed on the ice. She was named Defender of the Year in the 2018–19 season in the CWHL, the final season before the league folded.

But *hockey player* is only part of who Ambrose is and only part of what defines her happiness and success. That's a lesson she learned throughout the year after she was cut from the Olympic team, as she came to terms with the devastation of the loss. It's a point she emphasized in the Hockey Canada article she wrote. Once that story was out, it felt freeing. "[Hockey Canada] asked me to be vulnerable," she said years later in an interview. "They asked me to talk about these things in my life that I've wanted to very much block out. And a good chunk of them were caused by Hockey Canada. I wholeheartedly accept that. It was a big part of it. But in a way, I actually think it was one of the most healing things for me to do."

After the article came out, she heard from lots of people. The support was overwhelming, but so was dealing with some of the people who reached out to share their own struggles. Ambrose didn't have all the answers to give them. But it became just the first of many times she's been open about her mental health. That advocacy work is something she's just as proud of as her play on the ice, and it's something that will be part of her legacy when she finishes her hockey career.

The stigma around mental illness has lessened, but it still exists in the hypercompetitive world of professional sport. Ambrose pointed to the ability of an NHL player like Patrik Laine to be open about his mental health struggles, when in previous years, his absence from the game might have been masked as a physical injury. Athletes in other sports have spoken out, too, like American tennis star Naomi Osaka, who said she was struggling with depression and anxiety in 2021. For Ambrose, it comes back to treating athletes like human beings and reminding herself that, first and foremost, she's Erin Ambrose from Keswick, Ontario, a daughter, a sister, a friend, a proud aunt to her young nephew, and a dog mom to a cockapoo named Henry.

Returning to Montréal in 2023 meant another chance to be close to people who had done so much for her at her lowest point. It was also a chance to be a leader on a new team. That didn't necessarily mean having conversations with young players about what she'd been through. She planned to lead by example with grace and humility, qualities she'd learned from Poulin, the best leader she'd ever been around. But most of all, it was an opportunity to win. The Erin Ambrose trophy case included championships in the NCAA, the under-18 world championship, senior world championships, and finally, in 2022, the Olympic gold medal she'd always dreamed of earning. She was missing a pro league championship. Despite being part of a talented Les Canadiennes team in 2018–19, Ambrose had never won one of those. Now, in the PWHL, she'd have another chance to bring a championship to Montréal, a city that loves women's hockey.

It's one thing to win with the national team over a short tournament or even at the Olympics, when you've shed blood, sweat, and tears with the same group for eight months. But to win with the team you've competed with day after day in a league environment, when you've pushed each other in practice, sat on buses and planes during road trips, and shared so many meals together over a season? That's an opportunity Ambrose hadn't had in years, and it drove her on the ice more than anything else.

At the draft, Sauvageau used her second pick, seventh overall, to select Kristin O'Neill, a speedy and hard-to-play-against forward who'd starred alongside Stacey on Team Adidas in the PWHPA the year before. Like Ambrose, O'Neill wasn't a stranger to Montréal, having lived in the city specifically to train at Centre 21.02 ahead of the 2022 Olympics.

"I felt like I really developed as a player when I was there," O'Neill told reporters in the media room a few minutes after she was drafted. "That was just before centralization. I'm really happy to be back and working with Danièle and Kori Cheverie." O'Neill had carved out a fourth-line centre role on the national team, but in Montréal, she'd have a lot more opportunity to shine higher up in the lineup. Only five foot four, O'Neill built her game on heart and a never-give-up attitude.

In the third round, Sauvageau picked forward Maureen Murphy, who had just finished a successful NCAA career at Northeastern University. Premier Hockey Federation MVP Loren Gabel was still on the board, as were US national-team forwards Hannah Brandt and Hayley Scamurra. But Murphy had experience playing with a talented centre at Northeastern in Alina Müller. Knowing how to play with a skilled player like that was an early hint that Murphy could find a role on Poulin's wing. "I think it'll be really creative, aggressive, and hard working," Murphy said of the lineup she would join in Montréal. "I know Laura Stacey a little bit; I don't really know [Poulin] that well. I obviously know who she is. Being able to learn from them both on and off the ice as a person and a player is really exciting for me and something that I never really dreamed of happening."

Immediately after the Murphy pick, Sauvageau used her fourth-round pick to choose Dominika Lásková, a versatile Czech defender who could also play forward. The season before, Lásková had won a championship with the Toronto Six in the PHF. She became the first PHF player drafted into the PWHL. Lásková travelled from Europe to attend the draft and thought she might have to wait until the later rounds. She was shocked to hear her name called so early. Her Czechia national teammates proudly snapped pictures of her as she walked to the stage.

One of Lásková's best friends, forward Tereza Vanišová, learned she'd be reunited with her friend and Czech national teammate in Montréal a few rounds later. They'd known each other since they were thirteen years old. They had lived together in Toronto, where Vanišová had also played for the Six the season before. It wouldn't take long for them to decide they would live together in Montréal, too. "It's just amazing we can continue playing together," Vanišová said after the draft. "We always have fun, so I guess that will continue as well." Later, Sauvageau would say it helped to see that both of those players had responded so well to a Canadian coach in Carla MacLeod, the PWHL Ottawa head coach who also coached the women's Czech national team. Lásková and Vanišová would end up being two of five players from that championship-winning Toronto Six team to find their way to Montréal.

Dominika Lásková (right), who would be the first PHF player selected in the PWHL's 2023 draft, poses at the 2023 PHF All-Star Game with Mikyla Grant-Mentis, who would also find her way to Montréal during the inaugural season. (Richard Scott)

The goaltender that backstopped the Six to that championship, Elaine Chuli, was among that group of five. Chuli, who was drafted in the thirteenth round, gave the team a reliable netminder behind the starter, Desbiens. Like her new goaltending partner, Chuli was also an accountant by trade.

The team finished the day with the rights to fifteen new players. Not everyone was able to have their draft moment in person. Some were working other jobs and couldn't come to Toronto. Others weren't sure if the cost would be worth it if they were on the bubble to be drafted. One player, veteran forward Ann-Sophie Bettez, followed the draft while moving house back in Montréal. Bettez had played her entire career in the city, from CEGEP at Dawson College to university at McGill to the Montréal CWHL team to captaining the Montréal Force during the team's only season in the PHF. Throughout her hockey career, she also worked as a financial planner because hockey didn't pay the bills. Bettez was taken in the fourteenth round that day, giving her the chance to experience another era of women's pro hockey in the city.

At the end of the fifteen rounds, Sauvageau felt it had somehow both been a long day and gone by fast. Her team had done research on nearly 250 players in a short period of time, all in the league's first month of existence. "We really wanted to take the time to talk to agents, talk to players as well and see some sort of potential combination," the GM said after the draft. "It is a great day for women's hockey." Sauvageau also sent her thoughts to the women who sat through fifteen rounds without being drafted that day. Some would get training camp invites. Each team now had three players signed and the rights to fifteen more, but the collective bargaining agreement required each team to have at least twenty-eight players invited to training camp. The undrafted players still had lots to fight for.

Having a real draft meant some players would be going to cities that were brand new to them. Jillian Dempsey had played her entire career in a Boston jersey, but Montréal selected her that day. Likewise, Jill Saulnier had lived and trained in Montréal but wouldn't get the chance to stay in the city. She was hanging out at the snack table when New York called her name in the seventh round, fortieth overall. Her best friend, Jessie Eldridge, had gone to New York in the third round and was standing beside her when Saulnier learned she'd be following her. Eldridge was her first big hug. "I actually had no idea, to be honest," Saulnier told a reporter who asked if she knew she'd be going to New York. "The hockey gods were above me and picked me."

The draft had been on Saulnier's mind constantly leading up to the big day, all through Hockey Canada training camp the week before. It was the culmination of a dream, the next big goal she'd set after winning her Olympic gold medal in 2022. Always laughing and smiling, Saulnier said her goal on her new team would just be to have fun. "I am a veteran. I'm an older player now, so now I have the opportunity to bring the experience that I've had and just enjoy myself and play the game I love professionally," she said on draft day. "No one's done this before, so now I have a chance to lay the foundation for the future and enjoy it myself."

Saulnier was part of the talented Les Canadiennes team that fell short in the playoffs in 2019. When the CWHL folded, she wondered if she'd ever play another professional hockey game. That feeling bled into a long pandemic stoppage and a six-month off-season before the draft, waiting for this moment to be part of a team again. "We didn't really know, and waking up every morning not really knowing your fate in something that you love and essentially your livelihood has been really difficult," she said. "Now we get to wake up with a new jersey and a salary, and it's something pretty special. There's a lot of people that have paved this road before us.... They're the reason we're here today."

While the draft made the league more professional and draft day was exciting, it also meant big life changes for players. Some, like Saulnier, were in their thirties and would have to pick up and build a life in a new city. For her, it meant leaving a city she'd loved over the last few years and teammates she'd loved playing with. It's one of the difficult parts of professional sports, that in an instant you could leave the place and people you've come to love. But it was part of the world the players had fought for years to experience.

8
MADAME SAUVAGEAU'S VISION

November 2023
Montréal, Quebec

When she was a child, Marie-Philip Poulin decorated her bedroom door with a poster of Danièle Sauvageau. Every time she closed that door, she saw Sauvageau dressed in her RCMP uniform, standing behind the bench.

Poulin was nearly eleven years old when Sauvageau coached Team Canada to its first Olympic gold medal in 2002, a moment that sparked Poulin's own Team Canada dreams. Sauvageau was an idol, an icon in women's hockey in the country and especially in Quebec. Not long after that, Poulin got to meet her idol at a hockey festival. Sauvageau still remembers the moment when the girl and her mother came up to her at the event. "Bonjour, Madame Sauvageau," Poulin said. Sauvageau asked if she played hockey. She said yes. Sauvageau asked if she was a good player, and Poulin responded by saying she was okay—the same answer she would probably give to that question today.

It was the start of a bond that would run through Poulin's journey to Montréal as a teenager, to Hockey Canada, and finally to PWHL Montréal. Mentor and player don't have to say much to communicate and understand each other. After Poulin won her most recent

Olympic gold medal in 2022, she put it around Sauvageau's neck when she came back to Montréal. Asked what makes Poulin special, Sauvageau can't put it in words. You could say Poulin is a good teammate, and she works hard, and she has talent. All of those things are true. But that doesn't do her justice. "There's not that many athletes or human beings that you cannot just describe, and she's one of them," Sauvageau said.

When Sauvageau decided to open Centre 21.02 inside Verdun Auditorium, she envisioned it as the home of a professional women's hockey team. Sauvageau's career has spanned other sports, including short-track speed skating, where she was once a performance director. It was those experiences with other sports that showed her the value of having a high-performance centre, where the present and future can train together to develop the best of the best and where athletes are treated professionally, with everything they need under one roof. She decided to build one for women's hockey, and anyone who wanted to train there could move to Montréal and do so.

First, she had to raise money to build the centre. She knocked on doors, collecting enough capital to sign a year-long lease, then enough to put a dressing room together, and finally, enough to build a gym inside the centre. When the pandemic happened, Sauvageau was able to get permission for national-team athletes to stay on the ice during lockdown because it was a high-performance centre and the athletes were training for the Olympics. "It's been our home," goaltender Ann-Renée Desbiens, who moved to Montréal to train at the centre, said during the first PWHL season. "We sweated there. We had days we didn't know why we were still showing up because we didn't have a league, and we still did because [Sauvageau] had the vision for us to be able to keep growing and keep getting better. Verdun is special."

When the centre was under construction, Sauvageau brought Poulin for a tour. The CWHL had folded, and the league the PWHPA players had been fighting to create didn't exist yet. Walking around wearing steel-toed boots and hard hats, it was hard to see a clear picture of what Sauvageau had in mind. At that moment, it didn't look like an elite training centre for female hockey players. There wasn't even any ice. Poulin might have been a bit skeptical, but she trusted Sauvageau.

As she stood in that same rink in November 2023 during PWHL Montréal training camp, Poulin could clearly see the benefits of Sauvageau's vision. She spent many hours training at the centre before the PWHL started, working every day without knowing when this team and league might arrive. Now, Poulin saw staff bustling around the rink. She saw a dressing room specifically for her team and meals provided, all in the home Sauvageau built. The team's first camp opened a few days earlier, and like the draft before it, it felt like a new beginning.

It wasn't lost on reporter Jared Book that the camp's opening press conference was set up inside Verdun Auditorium a few feet away from a glass case filled with Montréal women's hockey history. There were pucks and sticks and jerseys featuring the Les Canadiennes CWHL team and various gold-medal-winning Olympic teams. There was a framed photo of the Les Canadiennes team that won the 2012 Clarkson Cup, in a season that saw forward Caroline Ouellette put up an astounding sixty-six points in twenty-seven regular-season games. Ouellette smiled in a framed magazine elsewhere in the display, posing alongside Sauvageau. There was the puck that Jessie Eldridge shot into the net with less than forty-three seconds remaining in regulation to secure the PWHPA championship for Team Harvey's earlier that year.

The day was all about where women's hockey in Montréal was going, but on the Habs Eyes on the Prize website, Book wrote about the impossibility of avoiding all the reminders of where the sport had been, from the championship banners inside the display case to the name of Centre 21.02, which honours the date of the first Olympic gold medal for Canadian women in 2002. That, too, was part of Sauvageau's vision: to remember where you've come from as you try to build the future. "It was my way to say if Montréal was chosen to be part of this new league, it's because there's a lot of people, media included, that created this environment where the fans could come to the rink. Obviously a lot more people than the players wanted to have a team here in Montréal," she said later. "I think it's important to recognize. That is our motto: to recognize the past to build the future."

Soon, they would have a new jersey to add to the display case. With only a few months to prepare for the first season, the league's leaders opted to wait to introduce team names and logos, so the team would be called PWHL Montréal all season long. A few days earlier, the league had unveiled the new team's jerseys: cream-coloured away sweaters, maroon for home, with a simple *Montréal* on the front.

The training camp was scheduled to last almost a month and a half, unusually long because so much time had passed since most of the players had laced up their skates for a competitive hockey game. Players across the league didn't get on the ice on the first day of camp. It was more like the first day of school: they met their new teammates and went through medical testing. The first week was also when Sauvageau got to see all the players she had drafted together for the first time. It's one thing to make a list on paper. It's another to meet players individually, to see them step on stage at a draft. But sitting on the wooden benches inside Verdun Auditorium, Sauvageau finally got to see her team, and her lifelong dream, start to come to life on the ice.

—

At PWHL Montréal's second week of training camp, players were on the ice every day. Head coach Kori Cheverie was in charge alongside her assistants, Alex Imbeault and Éric Houde. But on some days during training camp, there were as many as six coaches on the ice to work with players on special skills. They included skills coach Alex Tremblay and Noémie Marin, the CWHL's all-time leading goal-scorer and winner of four Clarkson Cups. Caroline Ouellette, who had recently been inducted into the Hockey Hall of Fame, and who couldn't be with the PWHL team full time because of her job with the Concordia University women's hockey program, also made an appearance.

Ouellette and Marin were players Poulin had looked up to when she moved to Montréal at sixteen. She remembers watching them lift weights at Olympic Stadium and being in awe of their work ethic and their drive to compete on the ice. They became like older sisters to her, taking her under their wing in a new city. Years later, she was still in awe of them. She knew they hadn't had this kind of professional experience when they played, and she was happy they still got to be a part of it in some way. "How lucky we are in Montréal to have such a great staff and people wanting to help us," Poulin said after practice one day. "Taking the afternoon off to come and do that with us, I think it means a lot."

As the players practised on the ice, the team's director of hockey analytics, Mikael Nahabedian, walked briskly around the rink carrying a phone on a tripod, capturing video of the Montréal team's drills. Marie-Christine Boucher, the director of business operations, could often be found popping into the rink in between lots of meetings as she took on the gargantuan task of the business side of running a brand-new team. During training camp, because the team had yet to hire a full-time public relations person, she also handled media requests.

For lots of players, this was the first time they played for a team with so many staff. That included twenty-seven-year-old Sarah Bujold, a forward who signed with Montréal as an undrafted free agent. She grew up as one of seven children in Riverview, New Brunswick, and forged a path to professional hockey through a standout career at St. Francis Xavier University (StFX) in Nova Scotia. In 2017, U Sports, Canada's governing body for university athletics, named her women's hockey player of the year. After finishing at St. Francis Xavier in 2019, Bujold was supposed to come to Montréal to play for Les Canadiennes. But her plans were thrown in a blender when the CWHL folded. Instead, she took a roundabout route to Montréal that included stops in Sweden and with the Metropolitan Riveters in the PHF. She was disappointed to not be chosen in the PWHL draft, but it meant she got to pick her own destination as a free agent.

Sauvageau already knew Bujold from her appearance on a U Sports all-star team that Sauvageau had put together years earlier, made up of the best university players from across Canada. The opportunity to play in a city closer to home, combined with Sauvageau and Cheverie's vision and the chance to play with players like Poulin, sold Bujold. Off the ice, it wasn't until she arrived in the city that she realized how beautiful Montréal is.

Bujold was nervous on the first day of camp, but she found it striking how welcoming everyone was, including Poulin and Laura Stacey, who made sure to say hi to everyone new. "It's been unreal," Bujold said in an interview a week into camp. "I think I've always been wanting to be in an environment that has that level of professionalism, that has that staff to be able to support the athletes in general. I've never really had skills coaches before. It's pretty cool to go on the ice with them and be able to work on certain things that you maybe are struggling with or can tweak just a little bit to get that extra edge."

Throughout the week, the team ran simulations of games, complete with a DJ and a ceremonial puck drop, to try to prepare players for the real thing. The team would head to Utica, New York, for preseason scrimmages against the other five teams soon after. For now, an intrasquad game tailored to feel like an actual game was the best way to see players in action. Cheverie watched first from the stands and then from inside a media booth at the top of the rink. Three key players—Desbiens, Stacey, and defender Erin Ambrose—were missing from the scrimmage while they rehabbed injuries. Ambrose observed the action at first from behind the glass, and then all three set up exercise bikes and pedalled as they watched.

It was team black versus team white. Poulin was on the black team, paired on a line with Czech forward Tereza Vanišová and rookie Maureen Murphy. Vanišová would score the team's only goal. They lost 5–1 to the white team. "I hate losing," Poulin said with a laugh after the scrimmage, adding that she still had fun. "It's part of the process. Part of the system. It's been fun. Obviously it's a quick hour. You want to play more." After the first few days back in a team environment, Poulin was struck by what the day to day was like. When she came in, her stall was ready. Her laundry was done. Breakfast was prepared. Then she got to go on the ice, lift, and have lunch after. Coaches had their own offices. "All of those things may seem very small to people, but to us those are big," Poulin said. "Those are big wins." She just had to worry about her own performance, something she'd never experienced in a professional league before.

Just as important was the ability to have a full week of practising with a team. To be able to spend so much time working on special teams and little details was something Poulin had been missing since

Les Canadiennes disappeared in 2019. "It's been a while since I've had the chance to play on a team, to create that culture, to create a team where we want to win a championship," she said. "You build towards that. Every weekend, you play a different opponent where you've got to tweak a couple things. Those are details I really miss in the game."

The league hadn't officially announced home arenas for all its teams yet, but everyone expected PWHL Montréal would play games in Verdun. The schedule hadn't been announced yet, either, so there was no date to circle on the calendar for fans. With the stands empty on this day, and so many puzzle pieces still to come together, it was hard to imagine how it could feel with the arena packed. Poulin doesn't like looking too far ahead. She tries to stay grounded in the present. But she was excited for that moment in this place that became like home. "I think you can tell that, here, it's a very special rink," she said. "It's an old one. We're going to make it our own."

At the end of the month, the league released its schedule for the first season. Each team would play twenty-four games split evenly between home and away. Not all home games were played in the team's typical home arena, though, as some NHL arenas would host neutral-site games. Perhaps most notable for people who followed women's hockey over the years was that these games were scheduled for every day of the week. In old leagues, games were only on weekends because so many players had day jobs throughout the week. A few weeks later, the league announced a list of equipment providers for the first season. Not only would players not have to provide their own equipment, but they'd get to be choosy about what brands they used.

The league's first game would be on New Year's Day at Toronto's Mattamy Athletic Centre, the old Maple Leaf Gardens arena site that had been renovated several years before to become home to the Toronto Metropolitan University (called Ryerson at the time) hockey teams. Toronto would host New York for that first game. Montréal would play half its home games at Verdun Auditorium that first season and another chunk at Place Bell, a ten-thousand-seat arena in Laval that had opened in 2017. The team would begin its season on the road in Ottawa on January 2 and would have to wait until January 13 for its home opener against Boston inside Verdun Auditorium.

As it prepared for the season to begin, the league hired more than one hundred employees in a short period of time, including a chief medical officer who helped write medical standards and employees who focused on things like player experience, marketing, and game operations. One of the most important employees was Amy Scheer, a veteran sports executive whom the PWHL hired away from the NFL in November 2023. Scheer became the league's senior vice-president of business operations. Scheer asked to put a pause on everything from broadcasting to team branding. The league would ultimately decide to wait to unveil team nicknames and logos until after the first season. Jerseys had been ordered months before in order to get them in time for January, so there wasn't time to get logos and team names on those for the start of the season. Board member Stan Kasten would later say that things would have gone a lot smoother had Scheer been around in the summer, when work started on pulling together everything needed to run a hockey league.

On the ice, PWHL teams made the first handful of cuts as news of the league's schedule emerged. Montréal released two goaltenders, setting their crease for the first season. Ann-Renée Desbiens would be the starter, and she'd be backed up by Elaine Chuli. Their third goaltender would be New Brunswicker Marlène Boissonnault, who previously played for Team Harvey's in the PWHPA. Her job would be one of the most difficult on the team. She practised every day like everyone else, but unless another player sustained an injury, she wouldn't get to play in a game.

After the first round of cuts, all six PWHL teams went to Utica, New York, for the pre-season camp. It was the first time coaches and general managers got to see their players in real games playing against other teams. Each team played three games, which all went to overtime and a shootout regardless of the score, so each team's staff could see how their players reacted in different game scenarios. Those games were the first indication of how physical the league would be. They were also an opportunity for the PWHL to test out different rules as it finalized the rulebook. One rule tested that week was dubbed the jailbreak rule. If a team scored while shorthanded, they would free their player from the penalty box. It was a fun way to encourage teams to cheat for offence on the penalty kill, and it showed the PWHL was willing to do things differently than the NHL.

By the end of the Utica camp, teams had to make their final cuts. They were allowed to keep twenty-three players on standard contracts plus three more on reserve. The reserve players also had a difficult job. They would practise every day like the rest of the players on the roster, and they could be called to sign a temporary contract at any moment, should an injury happen. They would not, however, be entitled to all of the same benefits under the collective bargaining agreement, including the monthly housing stipend. These were difficult decisions, the difference between someone's dream coming true and someone else's coming so close but not far enough.

One of the players vying for one of the last jobs on the roster for the Montréal team was twenty-eight-year-old Catherine Dubois. In the summer, Dubois had almost retired from hockey. She had played the previous season with the Montréal Force of the PHF, and when that league folded, she wasn't sure whether she had a future in professional hockey. She had made the Force on the fringes, and with more competition, securing a spot in the PWHL felt like a reach.

Dubois bought a condo in her hometown of Quebec City and settled into the family masonry business. Her father grew up playing hockey for Granby in the Quebec Major Junior Hockey League but had to change direction when he met Dubois's mother and they became pregnant six months later. He went back to Quebec City and started working for the family construction business. When their family grew to five children, he needed a bigger income and started building his masonry business. It wasn't a glamorous job, but it was successful.

Dubois started working for her father when she was ten years old, learning the value of hard work from an early age. Growing up, she'd wake up at five a.m. and go to work with her brothers and her father. As she got older, her job was to lug heavy cement bricks on her back up and down ladders all day, a job Dubois had never seen another woman do on a construction site. Hockey, which she'd been playing since she was four, was a place where she could have fun. Playing and training always came after work.

When hockey coach Isabelle Leclaire first saw Dubois play, she was so much more dominant than the other girls on the ice. *God, this girl is so powerful,* Leclaire thought as she watched her that day. Dubois looked like a train, powering through others at will. All the hard labour at the family business had paid off. Dubois also had a good shot and was physical, having grown up playing with boys. Leclaire could tell she had to restrain herself from using her five-foot-ten frame and taking penalties.

Leclaire met Dubois and her mother and liked them immediately. She was surprised when Dubois agreed to play for Leclaire's University of Montréal Carabins; Dubois had earned two gold medals with Canada's under-18 team and had plenty of opportunities to go to the United States. But staying close to her family in Quebec was a draw. Back then, Leclaire didn't know just how much impact Dubois, who would eventually become the Carabins' captain, would have on her program. Dubois showed up with a level of emotional maturity that Leclaire hadn't seen in someone who was only twenty years old. The player didn't know just how much impact the coach would have on her, either.

At first, they were in confrontation with one another. Dubois and Leclaire disagreed on the role she should play, and on how Leclaire managed her bench compared to what Dubois was used to in the past. But Leclaire found Dubois's honesty striking. Dubois never went behind her coach's back and complained in the dressing room. She came to her directly, and they had many conversations inside Leclaire's office. Sometimes, they'd spend forty-five minutes talking, and by the end, Dubois could admit she could see where her coach was coming from. She had an open mind, and slowly, her confidence in Leclaire grew. The coach tried to help the player realize that sometimes she pushed too hard, that her work ethic pushed her to extremes. And the player helped the coach understand what she needed to do differently to reach her. "I was there to listen to her," Leclaire recalled. "I spent a lot of time with her. I think that's maybe what she needed at the time. She needed somebody to talk to and to confront some ideas."

For her part, Dubois was impressed with her coach's humility. Leclaire's focus on Dubois as a person stuck with her. "She saved me as a human being," Dubois said in an interview during the first PWHL season. That relationship helped Dubois overcome setbacks in university, beginning with a serious kidney condition that hospitalized her in her first year. The health scare zapped her confidence and her strength. Leclaire was the first person who helped her open up about that, and Dubois started to learn that not everything could be fixed by pushing and working harder, as she'd learned growing up. "When we were young and with five kids, a lot of stress with the company, we were not very talkative," Dubois said. "We couldn't express our emotions. I grew up following the authority and never asking questions. I was doing whatever they would ask me to do. In hockey, too. Isabelle was the first one to listen to me and to make me realize that it's not only the result that matters."

When Dubois came to Leclaire later in her university career and told her she wanted to step away from hockey because she wasn't having fun anymore, Leclaire didn't immediately try to convince her to stay. She told her she was sad to see her leave, but if Dubois thought it was best for her personally, Leclaire would respect it, as long as Dubois knew that if she changed her mind, the coach was only a call away. A couple months later, Dubois called to ask if Leclaire would have her back on the team. Leclaire didn't hesitate. When Dubois came back, she was different. The time away seemed to have strengthened her love for the game. She didn't question herself as much, and she was happy to be there.

Those challenges helped prepare Dubois for the uncertainty of being a professional female hockey player. During the pandemic, with the CWHL no more and her future up in the air, Leclaire "was always there for me," Dubois said. Leclaire let Dubois practise with the Carabins to get some extra ice time. It gave her the chance to access coaching when she wasn't on a team and trying to compete with national-team players who had more resources felt daunting. In the summer of 2023, after the PHF folded, Dubois felt she'd reached the end of hockey. It had become impossible to prepare for the next year, and she wanted to build a foundation for herself moving forward. Hence the condo in Quebec City and working for the family business.

A call from PWHL Montréal general manager Danièle Sauvageau, who invited her to training camp in Montréal, changed everything. It wasn't a guarantee, but it was an opportunity. When Dubois had first thought of the prospect of making the PWHL team, she'd thought it was unrealistic. She needed to work in Quebec City, which meant she couldn't have access to ice and a trainer the way that players in Montréal did. How could she beat one of them for a spot? But when the call came from Sauvageau, Dubois decided she would find a way to make it work. She would grind like she always had and prove she belonged. She found herself driving back and forth between Montréal and Quebec City to keep working for her father while she fought for her opportunity in camp. She also picked up occasional shifts coaching and working at a hotel, all to make ends meet.

When the final cuts happened in December, Dubois wasn't one of the twenty-three players offered a contract. But she was one of the three players on Montréal's reserve list, meaning she could be called up if someone got hurt. Since Dubois would be earning less than the minimum league salary of $35,000, a friend offered to let her to stay in her Montréal apartment so Dubois would have a place to live in the city without having to pay for two homes. She knew that if not for the people in her life who supported her, she couldn't have kept playing hockey. It's that support system, and her ability to never give up, that makes Dubois most proud. If she counted the number of times she thought about giving up on hockey, she'd run out of fingers to count on. But something always burned inside her. She'd say she was done with hockey and then go work out the next day, as if the sport wasn't quite done with her yet. A part of her couldn't stop thinking about the idea that everything might work out.

—

With the final roster set and the schedule released, the countdown began to the beginning of the PWHL season on January 1. There were early signs of how much interest there might be in the league. At the Utica camp, word came that Toronto had sold out all of its home games on the day single-game tickets went on sale. It was the smallest rink in the league with a capacity of around 2,500 fans, and Toronto has always been a hub for women's hockey, but that it sold out so quickly was a bit of a surprise. Montréal's tickets were selling fast, too.

The team had one last thing to deal with before its first game: naming its leadership group, including the player who would wear the *C* on her sweater. At the end of December, the whole team went to a Cirque du Soleil *Crystal* show on ice. During the show, one of the skaters came out wearing a Montréal jersey with a *C* and the number 29 on it: Poulin's jersey. While no one was surprised to learn Poulin would be captain, she didn't know the announcement was coming during the show. A video posted by the team showed a wide smile appear on Poulin's face as she realized and pointed at the jersey. Her teammates smiled with delight, one ruffling Poulin's hair and displacing her trademark toque. Cheverie filmed Poulin's reaction with her phone. Later that day, the team officially unveiled Poulin as its captain at a press conference in Verdun. "She always puts others first," goaltender Ann-Renée Desbiens told reporters that day, "and I don't think there is any better person to be the captain of the first PWHL team in Montréal."

"A bunch of us are up here, but this team is all of us," Poulin said, adding how lucky she felt to wear the C.

Erin Ambrose and Laura Stacey would serve as assistant captains, while Kristin O'Neill would be an alternate assistant captain. Desbiens, defender Kati Tabin, and forward Ann-Sophie Bettez would also be part of the team's leadership group, even if they didn't wear a letter. Montréal players presented each other with their jerseys at a ceremony at the iconic Mount Royal. Days later, they'd begin a new era in Montréal women's hockey, a journey that would be bigger than any of them could have ever imagined.

9
DROPPING THE PUCK

January 1, 2024
Toronto, Ontario

The lights went dark inside the Mattamy Athletic Centre in downtown Toronto. One by one, PWHL Toronto players skated on to the ice. It was the team's first introduction to their fans in Toronto, including the 2,537 people who were in the stands, and also the introduction of a brand-new women's hockey league to the world. This was the first of seventy-two games that would be played in the PWHL's inaugural season. Toronto was facing off against New York. For many players, it was the first game they'd played in more than eight months that would count in the standings.

These teams had been built from scratch over the previous four months, from the staff making things run behind the scenes, to the equipment, to the players skating on the ice. Some of these players had sat out league play for the last few years, working to create something better. Some, like Toronto's Sarah Nurse, had played in the CWHL, toiling for little to no pay inside community arenas. Nurse became one of the players who negotiated the collective bargaining agreement that underpins this new league. Others played in the PHF, only to watch that league disappear overnight. For other players, this was their first professional hockey game. They didn't have to lug their own bags home at night or find their own meals. This would be the standard from day one for them, and their careers would look very different from the players who came before them. For all, it had been a long journey to get to this point. Standing on the blue line in her New York jersey was Jill Saulnier, who had wondered whether she'd play another professional game after the CWHL folded. Reserve players and third goaltenders, not guaranteed to see action this season except in the case of an injury, were dressed and on the ice for the ceremonial puck drop, too.

The sold-out crowd cheered as Billie Jean King, wearing a purple blazer and matching glasses, an ode to the league's colours, was introduced. Earlier that afternoon, King had popped into both the Toronto and New York dressing rooms to give the teams a speech before the first game. Now she held onto Jayna Hefford's arm. Hefford held back tears as she and King walked down the carpet. It was a moment that might have been hard to imagine in the three previous leagues where Hefford had played. A year before, sitting on a bench outside a rink in Florida, she'd told a reporter that she just wanted her kids to see her work hard at something she cared about. On this day, they got to see her reach that dream in person. An emotional energy hung over the rink all day, she said, and that moment with King, walking down the carpet and seeing the crowd and the players on the blue line, was when reality sank in for Hefford. The game always matters to professional hockey players, but on this day, it felt irrelevant. Hefford felt it was more about starting a new chapter.

Then Toronto captain Blayre Turnbull and New York captain Micah Zandee-Hart skated up for the ceremonial faceoff. King kissed the puck in her hand before both she and Hefford dropped their pucks, putting the final bow on the league King had believed in from that first phone call with Kendall Coyne Schofield more than four years earlier.

New York defender Ella Shelton made history when she scored the first goal in league history more than ten minutes into the game. It would also hold up as the game winner as New York blanked Toronto 4–0. Shelton's stick would be donated to the Hockey Hall of Fame, along with the first faceoff puck and the stick New York goaltender Corinne Schroeder used en route to her shutout. All four goal pucks are also in the hall, including the one Saulnier fired past Toronto goaltender Kristen Campbell for New York's third goal of the game.

The game was broadcast on CBC, TSN, and Sportsnet and reached nearly three million people, according to CBC. People didn't just tune in for the first couple of minutes, either. The audience peaked at 1.113 million during the second period. It was an encouraging first sign of what was to come that season. But everyone knew the first game would attract attention. The next challenge for the PWHL was to find a way to hang on to it.

One day after the emotional game in Toronto, it was Montréal's turn to play its first game. The players travelled to Ottawa for that team's home opener inside TD Place, a building that holds an important place in women's hockey history. It's where the Canadians won the first Women's World Championship in 1990.

The demand for tickets to that first Ottawa–Montréal game seemed to take the league by surprise. It opened up more tickets in December and those sold, too, filling 8,318 seats inside the arena. The game would set an attendance record for the most fans to watch a professional women's hockey game, beating the 7,765 who watched the championship game in the Swedish Women's Hockey League in 2022. The city that wasn't originally part of the PWHL's plan was off to a good, and very loud, start.

It wasn't just the volume of the crowd in Ottawa that was stunning. Early into the game, it became obvious that the league would be physical by virtue of officials allowing more contact around the boards. The first game had been physical, too, but this game turned it up a notch higher. It felt like everyone had gotten the memo that they could hit people.

With the game still scoreless in the second period, Montréal defender Dominika Lásková was called for tripping. The PWHL had opted to keep the jailbreak rule it had tested during the pre-season, which gave teams a bit more incentive to try to score during the penalty kill so they could free their player from the box. On the penalty kill, Montréal's Ann-Sophie Bettez picked a puck up off the boards and passed it to a streaking Marie-Philip Poulin, who had found open ice. Poulin skated past every Ottawa player toward the net until a sprawling Ottawa player tripped her. The whistle blew. Poulin was awarded a penalty shot. As she prepared for the whistle to blow to take the shot, the crowd started booing Poulin. The same people who would cheer for her in a Team Canada jersey now wanted her to miss. Inside the press box at TD Place, the strangeness of the booing didn't immediately sink in for reporter Jared Book, who'd travelled to Ottawa to watch PWHL Montréal's first game. Of course they're booing, he thought, because Ottawa is their team. Even though the team had only just started playing, and this was the first time these two teams had faced off, allegiance was already building among Ottawa fans. The booing was a good thing.

As the crowd booed, Ottawa goaltender Emerance Maschmeyer looked straight ahead. She'd faced lots of shots from Poulin when they played together on Les Canadiennes of the CWHL and on Team Canada, but this was their first battle in the PWHL. Maschmeyer made the save. Poulin wouldn't be the first player to score a goal in a

PWHL Montréal jersey. That honour would go to rookie Claire Dalton at the end of the second period.

By the midway point of the third period, Montréal trailed Ottawa 2–1. With a little more than five minutes left, Laura Stacey used a burst of her trademark speed along the boards to drive to the net, putting the puck past Maschmeyer to tie the game. The first player who came to hug her behind the net was Poulin, who drew the secondary assist on the goal. The photo of the two of them celebrating would become one of the most memorable from that first season.

About a minute into three-on-three overtime, the relentless Kristin O'Neill chased down Ottawa defender Savannah Harmon to win the puck back. O'Neill passed to defender Kati Tabin, who took a shot that an Ottawa player's stick broke up. The puck found its way to Bettez, who fired it past Maschmeyer. In PWHL Montréal's first game, the veteran who'd spent her entire career in Montréal, who hadn't been sure if her career would continue into this league, scored the game winner. It felt fitting.

Even though Ottawa lost, the crowd gave both teams a standing ovation at the end. The teams posed together for a photo at centre ice to mark the occasion. After the game, Jared Book interviewed an emotional Hayley Scamurra, who'd scored Ottawa's first franchise goal. The emotion wasn't necessarily because they lost the game. Book could tell it was more than that: players could feel a weight lift off them. They no longer had to answer questions about whether or not they chose to play in the PHF or with the PWHPA, or why the PWHPA's promised league was taking so long, or anything else around league building. They could focus entirely on hockey.

—

The Montréal team spent its first week of the season on the road. After playing in front of a record-breaking crowd in Ottawa, the team headed to Minnesota and New York.

The game in Minnesota was that team's home opener inside the Xcel Energy Center, where the marquee tenant is the NHL's Minnesota Wild. An NHL rink was a bit big for what the PWHL was forecast to draw in its first season, but that's where PWHL Minnesota ended up playing almost all its home games. Days before Montréal played Minnesota on that first Saturday in January, the game seemed poised to smash the attendance record set in Ottawa just a few days earlier. When the day came, more than thirteen thousand people were in the stands at Xcel. It broke the Ottawa record by almost five thousand people.

Advisory board member Stan Kasten was at the rink that night. It was the latest stop on a whirlwind tour that began for him on New Year's Day for the first game in Toronto. From there, he went to Ottawa on January 2, Boston's home opener on January 3, and finally, Minnesota for another record-breaking crowd. To put things in perspective, as a baseball executive Kasten had lost the World Series in three of those four cities. If you want to pick out the one that caused him the most pain, his Atlanta Braves lost the 1991 World Series to the Minnesota Twins in extra innings. To be that close and lose is the kind of thing that can haunt you for the rest of your life. That was on his mind during the tour.

Baseball trauma aside, Kasten was overjoyed when the first game in Toronto sold out. Then, Ottawa blew expectations out of the water. He knew Boston would be tricky. The team played half an hour north of the city in Lowell, a drive that can take a lot longer in traffic. Boston's home opener against Minnesota drew a little more than four thousand people. And then, to have more than thirteen thousand people in an NHL venue for Minnesota's home opener against Montréal? That was the moment Kasten knew the league had made it, that they'd gotten things right on the ice, even if they'd made mistakes in other areas. Still, it was early, and some within the PWHL wondered if the excitement might fade once the league was no longer new and shiny. It's one thing to draw a big crowd for the first game. What about a Tuesday night in the middle of February?

On the ice that night, the home crowd in Minnesota rewarded the more than thirteen thousand fans by shutting out Montréal 3–0, thanks to a hat trick by rookie Grace Zumwinkle in her first professional game in her home state. There wasn't much time for Montréal to linger on the loss. The team was headed home for a much-needed off day, and then back on the road again, this time bound for New York.

10
THE PAST, PRESENT, AND FUTURE

January 10, 2024
Belmont, New York

Catherine Dubois showed up at Verdun Auditorium on a Tuesday morning, only to find herself heading back home again to pack. She'd just learned she'd be travelling to New York for PWHL Montréal's third game of the season. With some players nursing injuries, Dubois might be needed to fill in. As she rushed home, she reminded herself not to forget to pack her passport. Dubois had been training with the rest of the team since the season began, preparing for the moment when she might be called upon to play. That day could have come a week into the season, a month into the season, or not at all. That's life for the players on PWHL reserve.

The PWHL's collective bargaining agreement spells out a long list of benefits for players who are on standard player agreements, including a monthly housing stipend and a minimum salary, among others. Teams could only have twenty-three players at one time signed to standard player agreements, typically running from one- to three-year deals, unless a player was moved to long-term injury reserve. For times when players are hurt or sick and can't play for a short period of time, the PWHL came up with the idea of reserve players. Each team could have a pool of up to three players to call upon at any moment to fill in for another player. When that happened, those players would sign a short-term standard player agreement. In that first season, a reserve player received a minimum stipend of $15,000 per season. For the time they were called up and under contract, they received a prorated amount of the $35,000 minimum salary and the housing stipend, equal to the number of days they were under contract. It meant the reserve players would work just as hard in practice as rostered players, since they had to be ready at any time, but they wouldn't receive the same compensation.

A team could call up a player on reserve for a ten-day contract only twice before it needed to sign them to a full-time contract to play again. It was designed that way to make sure the reserve players were only used for emergency situations, where an injury call-up was necessary. For a reserve player to get one of those twenty-three full-time contract spots, another player would have to be released or injured long-term. Dubois signed her first ten-day contract, but on the day she went home to pack for the road trip, she wasn't yet certain if she'd get the chance to play in the game against New York. Still, she was a mixture of happy and nervous. She felt ready. The next day, her chance came. With forwards Laura Stacey and Ann-Sophie Bettez out of the lineup nursing ailments, Dubois was told she'd be playing. She decided she'd enjoy the moment as much as she could, as if it were the one and only game she'd get to play in a PWHL Montréal sweater.

That night was another night of firsts in the league's opening month. Not only was Dubois the first PWHL reserve player to get called up to play a game, but it was also the first game inside UBS Arena, the home of the NHL's New York Islanders. PWHL New York split its home games between a couple of different arenas in that first season as the team looked for the best home and navigated arena availability. This meant having a second home opener, with Islanders legend Bryan Trottier on hand to drop the puck inside UBS Arena.

After Montréal was shut out the game before, questions started swirling in the media about the team's lack of offence. Some of that was pointed toward captain Marie-Philip Poulin, who hadn't yet registered a goal. It had only been two games, but for Poulin, expectations were always high. All the worrying was for nothing. A little more than eight minutes into the game, when Montréal was trailing 1–0, Poulin passed the puck from the neutral zone up to defender Erin Ambrose. Poulin found space to streak to the net, where Ambrose hit her with a perfect pass in the low slot. Poulin beat New York goaltender Corinne Schroeder stickside for her first PWHL goal, tying the game.

Even though it was Dubois's first PWHL game, it was obvious the league's physical style of play was right up her alley. Dubois had grown up playing boys' hockey. Having PWHL officials allow more physicality around the boards—even if everyone was still figuring out where the line was—suited her game. Her energy earned her a shot on the first power-play unit, where Stacey's absence created a hole in the lineup.

On a player advantage in the second period, Dubois headed immediately to the front of New York's net. She used her frame to screen the goalie—and occasionally shoved a New York player who tried to shoo her away. That's where she was when a scramble ensued in front of the net, and Dubois was able to hold her own to get her stick on the puck and put it past Schroeder for her first PWHL goal. For Dubois, the moment was surreal. Every time a player steps on the ice, they want to score. But she wasn't expecting it. Dubois's university coach, Isabelle Leclaire, happened to be an analyst on the French RDS broadcast that night. She felt so happy for Dubois that she could have jumped in the air. Knowing what Dubois had been through over the last few years and how difficult it had been for her to stick with hockey when the odds seemed stacked against her made it all a bit sweeter. After the game, head coach Kori Cheverie said she couldn't have asked for a better performance from Dubois in her first game. In what was looking to be a physical, high-paced style of play, Dubois's heavy game and ability to go to the net was needed, the coach said. "She's a fearless hockey player and that was something that our group really fed off tonight," Cheverie told reporters. "She had a major impact on the game." Montréal won the game 5–2, thanks to two more goals from Poulin to complete a hat trick. It was backup goaltender Elaine Chuli's first PWHL start and win. It had been more than nine months since she'd started a game in a league, but she didn't miss a beat.

Before the game, Cheverie had encouraged Poulin, who had registered only four shots in the team's first two games, to shoot a bit more. Poulin is a star, but she's never been a selfish player, always more eager to set up a teammate for a beautiful goal than to score one herself. Poulin took the coach's advice, and it paid off. She was named the game's first star. "Pou is obviously the heartbeat of our team," Cheverie said. "Everything that we asked the group to do, she does it. She's usually the first one to do it. And she's always competing with herself and her teammates with her details and habits. It was only a matter of time before she started filling the net."

For Dubois, the stellar performance was a great way to start her PWHL career, but she still didn't know how many of these opportunities she might get. Instead of wondering what might happen when her ten-day contract ended, she tried to focus on the positives and soak up every moment she got. She was lucky to come to the rink every morning instead of lugging heavy materials around a construction site.

After three games of firsts for three other teams, PWHL Montréal headed home. The team had been training inside Verdun Auditorium for three months now but hadn't yet seen the arena full of spectators on the wooden benches. They'd finally get to have their moment with their fans.

From the second you walked into the Verdun Auditorium on the Saturday of the team's home opener, you could feel the anticipation. Outside, the skies were cloudy, spitting out a mix of snow and rain all morning and afternoon. But inside the arena, people were lined up in the main lobby, waiting to be let in. Staff members buzzed around inside the rink, making final preparations before opening the doors.

Home opener day had been nearly two weeks in the making for PWHL Montréal, but for many, it felt longer than that. General manager Danièle Sauvageau had dreamed of this moment years ago. Laura Stacey had been training in Montréal for a couple of years but had never played a pro league game in a Montréal jersey in front of home fans. Erin Ambrose hadn't worn a Montréal jersey in nearly five years, and she'd come so far since her crushed Olympic dreams led her here. Marie-Philip Poulin had played at home a few times over the last few years in PWHPA showcases and with the national team. But this was different for her, too.

Two weeks into the league's first season, the public response had already surpassed senior vice-president of hockey operations Jayna Hefford's expectations. Smaller crowds in Boston and New York were a sign that the PWHL still had a lot of work to do to sell the sport, but Montréal was never in question. From the moment that Hefford and the players began thinking of what a league might look like, it had included Montréal. Hefford played many games in this city over her own pro career and was convinced it was a women's hockey city.

Before more than 3,200 people filtered into the rink to find their seats, Hefford talked to a big group of reporters—so many that it was a struggle to find room for every media member to set up inside the auditorium. She told the group that every aspect of the launch, from the attention it received in the media to the size of some of the crowds, had outperformed what she'd expected. But she was clear that the league still had work to do. There was undoubtedly a demand for women's sport, and if the league did things right, it could capitalize on that. Then she fielded questions about names and logos, telling reporters they were still working on those and didn't want to rush them. She also answered questions about what might be coming next, even though the league had existed for only two weeks. Could the league expand? What about a development system? The league didn't have a feeder system or farm teams where prospects could develop for the PWHL. In many cases, players developed in college, with most women not transitioning to pro hockey until they graduated. As teams drafted more players in future years, Hefford acknowledged, teams would need to find a way to keep them playing even if they weren't on the main roster. At the same time, Hefford said, the league didn't want to expand too quickly.

Montréal was hosting Boston for the home opener in Verdun, the first time those two teams were meeting. For Boston captain Hilary Knight, this marked a return to the city where she'd last played in a professional hockey league, having competed for Les Canadiennes until the CWHL shut down in 2019. Boston had only played one game so far—a loss to Minnesota in its home opener—and was still looking for its first win. A win in regulation is the most valuable thing in the PWHL. Unlike the NHL, the league awards three points in the standings for a regulation win, followed by two for an overtime win and one for an overtime loss. In a tight, six-team league, three points can make the difference between being one of the four teams in the playoffs and sitting on the outside looking in.

One of the fans inside the rink that day was Madelyn Delong, a fourteen-year-old girl whose family had driven more than eight hours from Fredericton, New Brunswick. The trip was a Christmas gift for Madelyn and her brother, but they'd made the long trip without knowing for sure if they'd be able to go to the game. Tickets had been sold out for a while, and the Delongs hoped they could find some to buy at the last minute.

When they showed up at the rink in Verdun the day before the game, they found the team practising. A reporter interviewed Madelyn. She watched Poulin speak to the same reporter, and then, to her surprise, Poulin came over to say hello. She gave Delong a signed stick, and the team helped the family find four tickets to the home opener. Now inside the rink, Delong still couldn't believe what she was seeing. She'd stayed up late to watch Olympic finals from faraway time zones, and now her favourite player was competing on the ice in front of her. The long drive was worth it. "Seeing the intensity, the atmosphere of the game, the competitiveness, the passion that goes through it, the girls on the ice love the game so much just like I do," Delong said that day. "But being able to see them get a professional league is so cool."

The volume in the auditorium climbed as PWHL Montréal players came onto the ice for the warm-up for the first time in their home arena, the type of rink where you feel almost on top of the action. The cheering continued as the players skated laps and shot pucks. At the end of the warm-up, Stacey and Poulin were last off the ice, piling pucks into a crate before two staffers came out to help them. Fans would see the pair do something similar before every game. They'd stay on the ice until the end of warm-up and collect pucks, and then Poulin would always have to flick one into a crate held by Stacey.

The lights went dark before the game began. Every member of Montréal's staff crowded onto the team's bench and was introduced to the crowd. Coach Kori Cheverie's name was the last announced, drawing the most raucous cheers.

First out among the players was starting goaltender Ann-Renée Desbiens, who smiled in the tunnel as she waited for the announcer to call her name. When it came time to design her mask for the season, Desbiens had included a drawing of retired goaltender Kim St-Pierre, one of her idols, along with Caroline Ouellette and Manon Rhéaume, carrying their gear through the snow toward the Verdun Auditorium. She wanted to pay tribute to the women who had worked hard for this moment but who wouldn't get to experience it as players. Before the game started, she had the opportunity to see St-Pierre who, Desbiens said, was so excited for the players that she had goosebumps.

After the goaltenders came the skaters. When Ambrose's name was called, she felt emotional. The highlights from the last six months played in her head, from the draft to training camp to the win in Ottawa. But this moment took the cake. Next was Ann-Sophie Bettez, who had wondered if she'd ever be a part of this league when it launched. She raised her stick to the crowd as she skated out, feeling she should appreciate every moment she got in this league, not knowing how long her career might last.

Catherine Dubois came soon after. Skating out in front of the sold-out crowd at Verdun Auditorium, Dubois had to pinch herself. In every game, Dubois was never certain of her status in the lineup until she got the green light. She hadn't thought she'd get to play in this game. She was grateful to Cheverie and the rest of the staff for giving her this moment in front of her friends and family. She'd called them at nine the night before to tell them she'd be playing and urge them to make the drive from Quebec City.

As the players skated out, they formed a circle around centre ice, facing out to the crowd, as a remix of Celine Dion's "The Power of Love" played. Last but not least emerged the captain, Marie-Philip Poulin. When her name was called, the crowd erupted, almost drowning out the announcer. Poulin looked a bit sheepish under the spotlight as she waved to the crowd and skated over to her players, fist bumping each and every one of them before taking her spot beside Desbiens. Once the players were all in place, they saluted the crowd.

Montréal and Boston players lined up on opposite blue lines as a red carpet was rolled out. Then, the crowd welcomed several women who had built the sport in Montréal, even if they didn't get to play in front of crowds this big. First was Hockey Hall of Famer Danielle Goyette, a forward from Saint-Nazaire, Quebec, who toiled in the Ligue régionale de hockey au féminin in her home province and later in the National Women's Hockey League. She was part of the first Canadian team to compete in women's hockey at the Olympics, taking home a silver medal before winning back-to-back golds in 2002 and 2006. Next was France St-Louis, a key part of a dominant era for Canada at the world championship, from the first in 1990 to the end of the decade. Kim St-Pierre joined them next. Another Hall of Famer, she played her whole career in Montréal, from McGill University to the Montréal Stars of the CWHL, where she mentored a young Poulin. After her was Caroline Ouellette, recently inducted into the Hall of Fame; arguably, she should have been there sooner. Some of the girls and women in the stands might have remembered all the goals Ouellette scored while wearing a Stars or a Les Canadiennes sweater or even joined her at the annual hockey camp she runs with Poulin. Last out was the general manager, Sauvageau. Her parents were in the stands to watch her that day, the first time both had been in the rink for a game since 2002. Sauvageau surprised Ouellette by bringing her two young daughters, Liv and Tessa, onto the red carpet. When Ouellette saw her children, she went back down the red carpet to them, picking Tessa up in her arms and taking Liv's hand, a smile on her face. Poulin and Knight joined the group at centre ice, the past, present, and future of Montréal women's hockey coming together as one. Liv and Tessa each dropped a puck.

Seeing that group walk out made Poulin tear up, maybe even more than when her own name was called. "They paved the way for all of us," Poulin said after the game. "We've watched them on TV going through thick and thin, and they battled hard to be able to play hockey. For us, for the fans to cheer them as loud as they did for them...they deserve it."

Sitting in front of the press room, reporter Jared Book felt the emotion, too. All night long, as he walked through Verdun Auditorium and soaked in the nervous energy of the first game, he saw familiar faces. There were people who'd volunteered with the old team. He thought back to calling games at the PWHPA showcase in this building in October 2022, when the stands weren't full. For years after the CWHL folded, and through a pandemic, and as he became a father, he'd wondered if he would still be covering women's hockey by the time this moment came. When the team took the ice, Book had one thought: the players did it. Best of all, his two-year-old daughter, Becca, got to take it all in from the stands with her mother, Shanna, who used to photograph the CWHL. Throughout that first season, Becca came to love going to PWHL games and cheering for her favourite player, Ambrose. She was still too young to grasp the gravity of the moment inside Verdun Auditorium that day. But unlike her parents, who'd had front-row seats to stops and starts in women's professional hockey, this world will be all Becca ever knows.

The crowd erupted every time a Montréal player touched the puck in that first game, beginning with Laura Stacey's shot less than a minute in. A drumline behind the Montréal bench kept things loud. The team killed off two back-to-back penalties called against defender Dominika Lásková, and the period ended scoreless. The rink felt packed during the intermission, with little room to move through the lane above the top row of seats.

Just thirty-three seconds into the second period, as some people were still finding their way back to their seats, the crowd got what it had been waiting for: Erin Ambrose shot a puck from the point past Boston goaltender Aerin Frankel for the first Montréal goal at home. Less than a minute later, Laura Stacey scored to make it a 2–0 lead. The crowd was elated, and when Boston defender Emily Brown took a roughing penalty two minutes later, Montréal had a chance to go up 3–0. On the power play, Marie-Philip Poulin found space and rushed to the net. She passed the puck back to Maureen Murphy, but Frankel stopped her shot. With the puck going the other way around the boards, Boston's Gigi Marvin, a veteran who'd walked away from hockey for a couple of years before coming back to play in the PWHL, pounced. She passed the puck to forward Taylor Girard, who was off on a breakaway. Girard beat Desbiens, slicing the Montréal lead to one goal and, thanks to the PWHL's jailbreak rule, freeing her teammate Brown from the penalty box in the process. A minute and a half later, in a moment of chaos in front of the net, Boston's Hannah Brandt tied it. Later, Kori Cheverie said her staff had focused on making sure the players didn't get too high or low on an emotional day. After the adrenaline of two back-to-back goals in front of a roaring home crowd, she thought the team got a bit too high, and it let Boston seize the momentum Montréal had built.

Montréal's second line of Stacey, Kristin O'Neill, and Tereza Vanišová generated good chances throughout the game—Stacey alone had nine shots. In the final minutes of the third period, Montréal had a golden opportunity to go ahead when Boston's top defender, Megan Keller, went to the penalty box for hooking, but Montréal just couldn't convert. The raucous crowd at Verdun Auditorium would get some bonus hockey.

Boston sent out Keller, captain Hilary Knight, and rookie Alina Müller to begin overtime, while Montréal called on their goal scorers that night, Ambrose and Stacey, along with Poulin. Montréal won the opening faceoff, and Ambrose took some time to regroup in her zone. She sent the puck forward to Poulin, who broke out of the zone and found Stacey rushing on the other side of the net. Stacey saw the puck and tried to get it as free as she could. Poulin tapped in Stacey's rebound just twenty seconds into overtime. It should have been a storybook ending on a night celebrating Quebec women's hockey, the captain coming up clutch with the overtime winner as the crowd cheered and the team rushed onto the ice to celebrate.

But that's not how it ended. As the Montréal players celebrated on the ice, Frankel shook her head. Knight spoke to the official, and Boston head coach Courtney Kessel filed a challenge for goaltender interference. From her vantage point, it looked like Stacey's stick pushed Frankel's pad back, putting the goaltender out of position to make the save on Poulin.

As the officials reviewed the goal, the crowd started chanting: "Goal! Goal! Goal!" It gave Stacey shivers on the bench. Then the referee skated out to centre ice and motioned that the goal had been disallowed. The crowd booed. After the high of celebrating a win on home ice, Montréal had to regroup and continue the game. A couple of minutes later, the puck came to Boston forward Amanda Pelkey, who was open to the left of the Montréal net, and she put the puck over Desbiens. This goal counted. It was over. The storybook ending at the home opener wasn't to be. Despite the outcome, the crowd gave the team a standing ovation, complete with "Montréal!" cheers.

After the game, Stacey told reporters she felt she was pushed into the net on the play that was ultimately deemed to be interference. But it didn't matter. "This moment is so much bigger than just one goal, one loss, one overtime loss for that matter," she said. "There's so much to it. Seeing the young girls, the young boys, all the fans in the stands today who've waited so long for this. And so did we."

Cheverie started her press conference with a statement in French, a signal to the community that she was serious about learning the language. A couple of minutes in, she was asked if she had looked at the disallowed goal again. She smiled and paused before answering, choosing her words carefully. "I mean, it's tough, right?" Cheverie said. "I was hoping that it was going to be a goal. It was obviously called off. I think everybody in our dressing room would disagree. But Boston's happy and leaving with two points." The disallowed goal, she said, seemed to take the wind out of the team's sails. But as professionals, they had to deal with adversity. It wouldn't be the last time they'd be faced with a call they disagreed with. Sometimes, she said, it was about momentum, but other times it was about the small details, like winning faceoffs. She felt that missing some of those small details ultimately cost her team the win. Poulin, who also thought the goal should have counted, thought the way the crowd reacted after the game spoke volumes. It's one thing for the crowd to be behind you when you win. But to stay and applaud when you lose? That's something special. "You wanted that win," Poulin said. "We went through a lot of emotion there, that minute and a bit in overtime. That's part of the game obviously, all the things you can't control. But we have to get back up for the next game."

The media room was packed with reporters and cameras that night. Having a full media room after games and sometimes having multiple reporters at practice, was an adjustment for players and coaches. It wasn't the norm for every PWHL team across the league, and it certainly wasn't the norm in previous leagues. But players like Ambrose also understood that the team needed the media to keep telling their stories and asking questions, even the hard ones. It was what players had wanted for so long, but it was all, as Ambrose put it, uncharted territory.

In a twenty-four-game season compressed into a few months, the players had to move on quickly. After practice Monday, the team had another game on Tuesday, this time in the ten-thousand-seat Place Bell in Laval. It would be a rematch against New York after Montréal's win at their first meeting earlier in the month. For players who hadn't played in a professional league with this kind of tight schedule in years, this too was an adjustment. The players were given Sunday off, a much-needed break after the emotional rollercoaster of the home opener the day before. Ambrose spent the morning with her family before they left town and then some time with her dog, Henry. Later she watched a game between Minnesota and New York; she's someone who's probably not going to miss a game unless she's playing at the same time. She also spent some of that day thinking about how the home opener had felt, even with the bittersweet loss. More than twice as many fans were in the bigger arena in Ottawa when they played there, but she felt Montréal was just as loud. To her, it felt representative of where the team was going and what made the city special.

Cheverie got to spend some time on Sunday with her mother, who was in town from Nova Scotia for the home opener. It wasn't an off day for PWHL Montréal's coaching staff, though. A quick turnaround between games meant days without practices were spent planning the next practice, making decisions on the next lineup, and scouting the competition. The coaches needed to make sure the players focused on what they were doing and not on the loss that just happened or what other teams were doing. "We try to stick to the same structure most days where we know by now that we only have one practice, max, to prepare for the next opponent and to get ourselves ready," Cheverie told reporters at practice on Monday after the home opener. "We're learning. It really takes consistency from our staff to make sure that every day, you come to work and it's a business first. Our players know that we care about them a lot. We've got a great relationship with them. But they also know that they have to come to work and we have to prepare. It's really just about consistency."

11
DANCING ON THE ICE

January 16, 2024
Laval, Quebec

The first game at Place Bell was on a stormy, slushy Tuesday night, not exactly ideal weather to convince people to brave the traffic from Montréal to Laval. Yet more than 6,300 people trekked more than thirty kilometres north of the city for PWHL Montréal's first game at Place Bell. It wasn't close to a sellout but, all things considered, a decent turnout.

The experience at Place Bell is different from Verdun Auditorium. For one, the arena's a lot bigger, seating more than ten thousand fans. It opened in 2017, and a lot of things feel new there, from the area set aside for media and broadcast to the amenities. As the seats filled up before the game began, general manager Danièle Sauvageau chatted by the glass with her New York counterpart, Quebecer Pascal Daoust.

The lineup that came out before the game included Catherine Dubois, who was nearing the end of the ten-day contract she'd signed earlier in the month. Asked about the situation the day before in practice, head coach Kori Cheverie had acknowledged how well the physical brand of hockey in the PWHL seemed to suit Dubois's game, and how she'd helped push back the other team and create room for Montréal's players. Throughout Dubois's career, she had been careful to avoid body-checking penalties. This season, for the first time, she could play her way. “We need players like that on our team,” Cheverie said. “They’re really hard to play against. We’re lucky that we have her with our group.”

But because players could sign only two ten-day contracts during a season before needing to sign a standard contract, and teams could only have twenty-three players at a time on standard contracts, Dubois’s future looked unclear.

Also in the lineup was Gabrielle David, a rookie pro who’d struggled when she was scratched for the home opener, especially with her family from Drummondville, Quebec, in the stands to see her play. After her solid career at Clarkson University, Montréal had selected David in the ninth round of the draft. David didn’t waste time in the game against New York in showing why she should stay in the lineup. She won a foot race to the puck and then scored from the slot when the puck found its way back to her. David’s captain, Marie-Philip Poulin, had been the first to speak to her after she got scratched in the last game, and she made sure to hug David after she scored.

By the midway point of the third period, the game was tied 2–2. It looked like it could be yet another overtime for Montréal, missing the valuable extra standings point that came with winning in regulation. With a little more than six minutes left, Poulin deflected a puck past New York goaltender Abbey Levy in front of the net. This time, Poulin’s game winner counted, giving Montréal a 3–2 victory and three points for the regulation win. Poulin was named the game’s first star, and she got a bit emotional in an interview shown on the arena’s video board afterward. Later, she told reporters that seeing how many people came to the game in Laval on a stormy Tuesday night had moved her.

It was the team's first win at home and the debut of their win song, "Le bal masqué." As the players celebrated, David, Ann-Sophie Bettez, Sarah Bujold, and Mariah Keopple debuted a choreographed dance at centre ice. They alternated skating arm in arm and ducking under their teammates' arms. The cast of characters in the routine would rotate throughout the season, but the dance at centre ice became a tradition for a home win.

As some players fought for a spot in the lineup, others adjusted to their roles. That included rookie forward Maureen Murphy. First was the adjustment from college to professional hockey. Murphy put up fifty-five points in thirty-three games in her final season at Northeastern University as part of a dominant line that also included New York forward Chloé Aurard and Boston's Alina Müller. But college hockey isn't nearly as physical as the PWHL. Then, there was the adjustment to a new city where she didn't know the language and or more than a few people, in a passionate hockey market where every lineup decision was under scrutiny.

Murphy found herself playing on a line with Poulin and Tereza Vanišová throughout the beginning of the season, something she admitted felt a bit surreal to her. Murphy grew up in Buffalo, New York, watching Poulin score against the Americans in Olympic gold-medal games. She also had a front-row seat to Vanišová's skill in the Hockey East conference, when Vanišová was playing at the University of Maine and Murphy, then at Providence University, had begun her college career. Murphy looked up to them as not only players but also people. In that first month of the season, Murphy had to remind herself she was good enough to play on that line. It wasn't that her teammates did anything to make her doubt that. The imposter syndrome came from within her, and she had to work to make herself believe she deserved her place. Poulin helped. Before the away game in New York early in January, she texted Murphy a quote, a reminder not to let herself get down if she felt she couldn't immediately compete with women who'd been pros for years: "Don't compare your chapter one to someone else's chapter twenty."

"Honestly, if she wasn't talking to me and telling me that I could do this and sending me quotes before and after games, I wouldn't have any confidence, because I would be too nervous to play with her," Murphy said in an interview after practice one day in January. "I'm most impressed with her leadership skills. She obviously is competitive, and we all get mad when we lose, but her ability to not let it affect her and still be a great leader is something I hope I can learn and eventually be in the future."

One of the things that makes Poulin great is her unpredictability on the ice. For Murphy, playing with Poulin was about trying to learn her tendencies, and that's something that could only be developed with time logged together. "I can't give her a bad pass, so that helps," Murphy said with a laugh. Coach Kori Cheverie also tried to keep Murphy focused on the present and thinking less about who she would be playing with each night. The tough part about playing alongside Poulin is that you're certain to get every opposing team's top players matched up against you every time you go on the ice.

On days when the team was at home but didn't have a game, Murphy was usually finished at the rink by one or two p.m. Then she'd set out to visit a new coffee shop and work on homework for her law degree. Murphy was taking two classes on top of being a professional hockey player, with the hope of eventually focusing on health-care law. She'd graduated with a master's degree in public health from

Northeastern University. She found herself working in health care during the COVID-19 pandemic, doing outreach work that included calling people to encourage them to get vaccinated. The experience showed her the problems in the American health-care system and, after she took a health law class, convinced her that she might be able to help people if she had a law degree.

When she wasn't studying or training, Murphy volunteered in the community, something she didn't advertise throughout the season. She would take her dachshund, Bean, to two different geriatric health-care centres. They'd visit seniors with dementia and Alzheimer's disease. Murphy would play bingo and Bean would get treats, especially from one resident who loved to share their ice cream. Murphy was drawn to volunteerism because of her background in health care but also because her grandmother was in a long-term care home. When Murphy was home, she would take Bean to visit her grandmother, and she liked the thought of a volunteer spending time with her grandmother when she couldn't be there. Murphy and Bean also visited adults with cognitive disabilities through a Best Buddies program, and Murphy helped with an elite girls' hockey team. Signed for three years in Montréal, Murphy found the volunteering helped her connect to her new community. It was also a good distraction from hockey, reminding her that she's a person first and can find joy no matter how she plays. She'd love to play hockey for the rest of her life, but she knows that's not realistic. Her volunteer work reminded her of life beyond the rink. "When hockey's great, it's going great," Murphy said months later. "But we all have those days where you don't have a good game and it's hard. Just having something else to do, if it's a way I can give back and help other people, it makes me feel content and like I accomplished something, instead of just relying on putting a little rubber disk in the back of the net sometimes."

—

Ann-Renée Desbiens marched into Jacques-Lemaire Arena, dressed in full goalie gear except for her skates and singing "The Wheels on the Bus." Behind her, Kori Cheverie, lugging a hockey bag, couldn't help but smile at Desbiens's singing. It was a Friday morning a little more than two weeks into the season, the day before the first matchup between Montréal and Toronto. They were set to face off inside Verdun Auditorium on Saturday night.

It's safe to say a field trip wasn't in Cheverie's practice plan. A malfunction at Verdun Auditorium meant the team had to pile into a school bus, gear and all, and lug everything to Jacques-Lemaire, a community rink in LaSalle, about a fifteen-minute drive from Verdun. But practice had to go on, and the disruption didn't seem to faze the players. If anything, taking a school bus was fun. "It's probably a coach's nightmare," Cheverie said that day. "But they just have a lot of fun with each other."

With Desbiens in front, the players walked through the arena named in honour of the famous hockey player and coach and down the steps, past the folding seats painted Montréal Canadiens' bright blue and red and all the way to the bottom, where they put on their skates and took the ice. The team focused on their power play, having converted just once on sixteen opportunities with the advantage in their first five games. The poor result came as a surprise for a team that built part of its identity around its offence. The issue, Cheverie said, was chemistry and execution. The power play had gotten opportunities. Finishing them was a challenge. Toward the end of practice, several men walking through for a lunchtime beer league game stopped to watch the pros.

Taking reps on the penalty kill that day was Leah Lum, who was coming off a game in which she'd scored her first career PWHL goal, an achievement made even more special because her brother was in the stands. Lum had taken a winding road to get to her first PWHL goal. It started in Richmond, British Columbia, where she grew up, then the University of Connecticut, where she played with future Montréal teammate Elaine Chuli. She went pro in the CWHL's final season, playing for the Shenzhen KRS Vanke Rays, one of the two teams based in China. Lum has Chinese heritage, but she had never been to China before the opportunity to move there to play professional hockey.

After the CWHL folded, the team moved to the Russian Zhenskaya Hockey League, and Lum stuck with it. That decision took her all the way to the 2022 Olympics, where Lum represented the Chinese team and served as an assistant captain. She returned to North America in 2022–23 and won a PHF championship with the Toronto Six. Being one of five players on the Montréal PWHL roster who came from that championship team, including Chuli, made the transition easier. "Everyone loves each other," Lum said after practice at the rink in LaSalle. "It's been unreal. I can't really put it into words how it's been. It's a very team-oriented, family-first type of thing in the locker room." That season, Lum was one of only a handful of players of colour in the league and one of only two Asian women—important representation in a sport that has historically been overwhelmingly white.

The spot on Montréal's roster was a position she'd had to fight to earn. Lum wasn't drafted. She made the team as a free-agent invite, helping her case by being a versatile player who can play forward or defence. She started her career playing hockey with boys as a defender and learned how to play forward when she switched to girls' hockey. Throughout her pro career and her time on the Chinese national team, she'd always played both. "I definitely do like the defensive side of things because you can see the whole ice, and I think that just comes from me starting out as a defenceman from when I first started hockey," Lum said.

A couple weeks into the season, Cheverie was mostly deploying Lum on defence. The coach liked her consistency and her ability to move the puck smartly. Cheverie told reporters that day that Lum would likely play defence going forward. But there were other decisions for the coach to make ahead of the first matchup against Toronto, including whether to put Catherine Dubois in the lineup for the last game of her ten-day contract.

Montréal versus Toronto on a Saturday night is the kind of matchup that players dream about playing in as kids watching *Hockey Night in Canada*. It was another sellout crowd inside Verdun Auditorium, where the ice issues from the day before had been fixed, and the first of several tough matchups between these two teams. Toronto was in last place in the league after a difficult start, but Montréal certainly wasn't taking the team any less seriously.

On the coaches' side, Kori Cheverie faced off against Troy Ryan. The two Nova Scotians know each other well and coach together on the national team. Both fought hard to get to where they are, coming from a small province. Ryan, one of three male head coaches in the PWHL, had used hockey to find a path out of poverty in Spryfield, Nova Scotia, finding male role models in the game.

Cheverie put Catherine Dubois in the lineup as the thirteenth forward, and Ann-Renée Desbiens got the start between the pipes. She was used to taking shots from several Toronto players who were also on Team Canada. In the first period, third-liner Sarah Bujold opened the scoring for Montréal off a pass from Leah Lum. But Toronto rookie Emma Maltais gave her team some momentum when she and Marie-Philip Poulin took penalties for some rough stuff in the corner. That delighted a few rows of the Verdun Auditorium that fans had transformed into a Toronto cheering section, including some of Maltais's family from Quebec. They waved cardboard cutouts of players' heads and an Emma Nation sign that usually hung in Toronto's home rink.

The game went back and forth through the first two periods, with Poulin adding another goal for Montréal. Every Montréal fan held their breath in the third, when it looked as though Poulin went off in pain but then came out for her next shift. Not long after, with a delayed penalty called to Montréal, Toronto's Natalie Spooner scored to give her team a 3–2 lead. On the next shift, Cheverie pulled Desbiens for the extra attacker. With a little more than thirty seconds on the clock, Poulin picked up the puck off the boards in the neutral zone. She carried it across centre ice, down the opposite side boards into Toronto's zone, and through three Toronto players to the net. She beat Toronto goaltender Kristen Campbell and tied the game.

There are moments where Poulin can make you wonder if what you just saw was real. That was one of those moments. In the press area, reporter Jared Book watched it unfold. He'd seen Poulin play for years, and even he never ceased to be amazed by what she could do. He couldn't help but smile. On the ice, Erin Ambrose, who was credited with the assist on the goal, just shook her head. "The girl is just built different beyond belief," Ambrose said after the game. "She is the best captain, the best leader, I've ever had. Marie-Philip Poulin is, I would say, the greatest female hockey player to ever play this game."

A little more than a minute into overtime, Toronto captain Blayre Turnbull was called for slashing, creating a golden opportunity for Montréal to win the game. Poulin had two good looks on Campbell, including one shot that seemed almost certainly in before Campbell got a glove on it. But again, Montréal couldn't execute on the power play. The game went to a shootout, and Toronto took an early lead off a goal from Hannah Miller. The PWHL has no limit on how many times a team can send out a player in a shootout. Cheverie sent Poulin out four times. Why not send out a player with two goals already in the game and who happens to have a reputation for being extremely clutch in these moments? "Why not? Best player in the world," the coach said after the game when asked why she turned to Poulin so many times.

But the captain scored just once on her four attempts. That left the game in the hands of Toronto defender Lauriane Rougeau, a shootout specialist who happened to be playing in front of her hometown crowd, and lining up against her friend from her youth, Poulin. Rougeau buried the puck, giving Toronto the two points.

After the game, Ambrose said it felt like her team stole a point. Montréal gave up forty shots, and their defensive coverage was lacking at times. She took accountability for turnovers on the power play. The team not only squandered a power-play opportunity in overtime but in the final ten minutes of the third period, too. Part of it, she said, was a reflection of a brand-new team having to come together so quickly. "We're going to get one," Ambrose said. "I know we are. We're starting to get some more reps, which is good in practices. It's something that takes time. I think you can throw a power play together and get a goal here and there, but that's also not sustainable. I think we're kind of building from the ground up and [it's] something that I do think is going to start to turn around."

The game was only the first of five meetings between Montréal and Toronto in the first season, and it would not be the last time Montréal would struggle to come out on top of that rivalry.

12

BATTLE ON BAY STREET

February 2024
Toronto, Ontario

The first month of the PWHL saw more than 106,000 people attend games across the six teams. What they saw on the ice was a more physical game than many predicted—which players seemed to like, though the line separating permissible play from a penalty wasn't always clear. Attendance records fell in Ottawa and Minnesota, where more than 21,600 fans combined attended. The month ended with Minnesota and Montréal tied atop the standings.

But there were hiccups in that first month, too. Poor weather postponed a game between Boston and Ottawa, one of the challenges when teams have to fly commercially. Before the season began, the media reported on several potential team names that emerged through trademark filings, and fans online promptly rejected them, feeling they were uninspired and didn't represent PWHL cities. Others were upset when the league opted to pause the introduction of team names and logos for the first season, after deciding to put more thought into team identities. The league couldn't keep up with the initial online demand for merchandise, though that might have been a good problem to have. One thing seemed certain, though: interest in the league didn't seem to be waning, even as it became less shiny and new as time went on.

Women's sports were basking in a long-overdue spotlight, and it wasn't limited to the PWHL.

National Women's Soccer League teams were seeing record valuations. The Women's World Cup in soccer drew more viewers than ever in the summer of 2023. While the PWHL was breaking records every month, a college basketball player named Caitlin Clark captured the world's attention. That came after record viewership for March Madness in 2023, when Angel Reese's Louisiana State team won. A year later, an average of 18.9 million people watched Clark's Iowa team lose to South Carolina in the final—more than 4 million more than those who watched the men's final, smashing the March Madness viewership record.

A July 2023 report from Nielsen found a growing appetite for watching women's sports, but lack of access to live broadcasts was a barrier. There was some proof of this in women's hockey. People came in droves every four years to watch the Olympic gold-medal game. When Canada defeated the United States in Beijing in 2022, a peak audience of 2.7 million tuned in on CBC/Radio-Canada, even though the game didn't begin until eleven p.m. Eastern. The American broadcast of the game on NBC averaged more than 3.54 million viewers, more than any NHL game in the United States that season. And yet those same people didn't show up when those same women competed in the CWHL or the PHF or any league that came before it. The PWHL tried to make the games easy to find in the first season. In Canada, CBC/Radio-Canada, TSN/RDS, and Sportsnet all aired games. The league also streamed every game for free on YouTube, where fans could talk about the game in a live chat. Sometimes players who were scratched for a game joined in. The league moved away from free broadcasts on YouTube in its second season, but it helped draw more fans in season one.

In a market like Toronto, getting to see a game in person remained a challenge. When all of the team's home games sold out even before the first season began, the league moved the February 16, 2024, game between Toronto and Montréal to Scotiabank Arena to try to get more fans through the door. The home of the NHL's Toronto Maple Leafs can seat more than 19,000 fans. If the Toronto game sold out, it would easily break the 13,316-person attendance record set in Minnesota. The league dubbed the game the Battle on Bay Street, a nod to the arena's address at 40 Bay Street in downtown Toronto.

Tickets went on sale a few days after the Battle on Bay Street was announced and sold out in less than half an hour. To put that in perspective, the CWHL held its all-star game at the same arena in 2017. The event drew 8,122 people, which set an attendance record for the league at the time. The PWHL was set to more than double that. Jayna Hefford, the senior vice-president of hockey operations, played her entire career in the greater Toronto area but never saw that kind of interest in a women's hockey game. She was blown away when the tickets sold out so quickly.

Montréal head coach Kori Cheverie also played her career in Toronto in the CWHL, and she had spent some months working as a video coordinator with the Maple Leafs a few seasons earlier. She grew up cheering for the Leafs, and now she would get to coach inside the rink where they play. The game would also be special for Laura Stacey, who also grew up cheering for the Leafs. While playing boys' hockey in Kleinburg, Ontario, a community in the city of Vaughan, her idol was Leafs forward Gary Roberts, who wore the same number, seven, that Stacey wore. It wasn't until the Canadian women won Olympic gold in 2002, when she sat in her living room and watched as a gold medal was placed around captain Cassie Campbell's neck, that Stacey saw women playing the game at a high level. Campbell became an idol, too, because that moment opened Stacey's eyes to what she could accomplish in women's hockey.

The Leafs will always be close to Stacey's heart. It's in her blood. Her number seven is also the same number her late great-grandfather, King Clancy, wore. Clancy won three Stanley Cups and was the highest-scoring defenceman in NHL history when he retired in 1936 after playing seven seasons for the Leafs. After retiring as a player, he became a coach and executive in the organization. A banner bearing his name and number hangs from the rafters inside Scotiabank Arena. While Stacey had competed in a three-on-three women's hockey challenge in the arena during NHL All-Star Weekend that year, the thought of playing a league game on that ice, beneath her great-grandfather's banner, gave her shivers. She knew it would also be a special moment for her family. "Obviously a lot of my family are pretty big Leafs fans, but I know as soon as Montréal gets into that building, their alliances are definitely shifting, and they're cheering on Montréal, which is pretty special to feel and to hear," Stacey said a few days after the tickets to the game sold out. The fact that the game was a regular-season contest, on any old Friday night in February, made that it sold out so quickly even more special. Like Hefford and Cheverie, Stacey played in the Toronto area in the CWHL, but she never had that many fans in the stands. When she scored the game-winning Clarkson Cup championship goal for the Markham Thunder in 2018 in Toronto's Coca-Cola Coliseum, which seats fewer than nine thousand people, the seats weren't full. Selling out Scotiabank Arena was a sign that women's hockey could generate lots of interest outside of big tournaments like the Olympics.

"In my career, I don't think league games have ever sold out to the extent that they are now and making history in terms of breaking record after record for a regular-season game," Stacey said. "Not for a championship. Not for playoffs. For a regular, everyday Toronto–Montréal game. I think that's why we sat out for so long. That's why all of the people had a hand in putting this league together because there is something more."

But before Toronto and Montréal could battle on Bay Street, Montréal travelled to Boston for a February 4 game in which Stacey scored the game winner in overtime off a perfect pass from defender Erin Ambrose. Then the league paused for nearly two weeks to allow for international play, including the Canada–US Rivalry Series. When the league resumed, Montréal's first game would be under the bright lights of Scotiabank Arena.

Before taking the ice against Toronto, the Montréal players got to practise on the Scotiabank Centre ice. The whole Montréal team walked through the rink where they'd be playing in a few hours. It would be the biggest crowd they'd ever played in front of, and Marie-Philip Poulin wanted to make sure they soaked it all in. She wondered how long it took to put white towels on every single one of the more than nineteen thousand seats.

Poulin and Laura Stacey were on their way to the media room before the game when Poulin spotted a familiar face. A giant portrait of Stacey's great-grandfather, King Clancy, hung outside the room. She urged Stacey to take a photo, but Stacey declined. Poulin wouldn't take no for an answer. She turned to a couple of photographers and asked them to take a picture of Stacey with Clancy's portrait. Stacey smiled for the photo, even if she was a bit embarrassed by the attention. Speaking to reporters, Stacey acknowledged how exciting the

At Marie-Philip Poulin's urging, Laura Stacey poses with a portrait of her late great-grandfather, King Clancy, at Scotiabank Arena. (Karissa Donkin)

moment was. But she also wished for a day when they weren't having so many firsts, when a crowd of more than nineteen thousand watching a women's hockey game was just the norm.

It would be the biggest crowd Kori Cheverie had ever coached in front of, too, and her priorities on that day were to try to keep players in their routines and to manage the excitement of the day. "It's definitely a pretty exciting building to be in and to be on that ice," Cheverie said before the game. "It's very bright. I'm just excited to see it filled with people." As much as she was excited to see the crowd, the coach was laser-focused on stick details and following the team's game plan. No one on the team had forgotten that the last game against Toronto had ended with heartbreak in a shootout. Montréal wanted to come out on top of the rivalry this time. But they faced a Toronto team on a three-game winning streak. Toronto had struggled to find a rhythm early in the season, and goalie Kristen Campbell took a while to find her confidence. In a game against Ottawa, Campbell was pulled after the first period when she allowed three goals on eight shots. The shootout win over Montréal a week later in Verdun had been a turning point for Toronto and Campbell.

A few hours later, PWHL fans filled the Scotiabank Arena concourse. Some wore PWHL jerseys. Others wore jerseys from Toronto-area teams of the past, like the Toronto Six of the PHF or the Markham Thunder of the CWHL. Some wore Hockey Canada jerseys. Many lined up at merch stands set up throughout the arena, where the league was selling Battle on Bay Street pucks and shirts. Then, as the lights dimmed, tiny light-up bracelets given to fans before the game glowed to life, and the arena shimmered white. A video with highlights from the league's first month was projected onto the ice.

WNBA star Kia Nurse dropped the puck in the ceremonial faceoff between her cousin, Toronto's Sarah Nurse, and Poulin. As they took their places for the opening draw, Poulin told defender Erin Ambrose, from nearby Keswick, Ontario, to take it all in.

The Toronto crowd was loud whenever their team had the puck, mixing cheers of "Let's go, T-O!" with its roars. But the game remained scoreless through the first two periods. Montréal had four power-play opportunities during those frames but again couldn't score. Toronto rookie Jesse Compher finally opened the scoring a little more than five minutes into the third period when she was left open in front of Ann-Renée Desbiens. It was her first career goal. Not long after, the attendance flashed on the video board, to the delight of the crowd: 19,285. A new record.

With less than five minutes left, a bouncing puck on a clearing attempt made its way back into Montréal's zone, and Toronto forward

Hannah Miller took a shot from just beyond the slot. As Miller fired, Montréal defender Catherine Daoust went down to block the shot, but she was a few inches off. The puck sailed past her and under Desbiens's right pad to make it 2–0 Toronto. For Miller, it was a heck of a way to celebrate her twenty-eighth birthday.

Cheverie called a timeout so her team could try to regroup. When the game resumed and Montréal got the puck out of their zone, Cheverie pulled Desbiens for the extra attacker. But Toronto's Victoria Bach poked the puck away from Ambrose and fired it into the empty net to make it 3–0. That would be the final score, though it didn't quite reflect how tight much of the game had been.

After the game, Cheverie said she felt her team had better chances on the power play this game, even if they failed to capitalize on all six opportunities. Montréal outshot Toronto, and Cheverie felt the team's defensive play had improved. But a missed assignment here and a bouncing puck there made all the difference. "It's important for our group to understand that they've got to be students of the game," she told a packed media room. "We preach that a lot, that every decision that we make matters. Getting a puck two inches over the blue line is just as important to us as coaches as putting the puck in the back of the net at times, depending on the circumstance. We're getting there, with our group, learning those moments. These games, although you don't like to lose, there's so much learning in them." Ambrose was asked about the power play, too. She also felt the team had had good opportunities but that Toronto's goaltender played well. Eventually, she said, one of those bounces would go in.

After playing in front of a crowd of more than nineteen thousand, the Montréal players and staff couldn't help but think about what a game inside their city's Bell Centre might feel like. Given its capacity of more than twenty-one thousand, a sold-out Bell Centre game could beat the record set in Toronto, and for a group of highly competitive people, it was a tempting thought. "I wouldn't be surprised if our GM is doing some things to try and make that happen," Ambrose said after the Toronto game. General manager Danièle Sauvageau was indeed working alongside the Montréal Canadiens behind the scenes to secure a PWHL game at the Bell Centre, though it would take a bit longer for all the details to come together.

It had been a busy February for Montréal's national-team players. They began the month playing with their PWHL teams, then many took part in NHL All-Star festivities in Toronto, followed by three Rivalry Series games in western Canada and Minnesota, before resuming the PWHL season in mid-February at the Battle on Bay Street.

The schedule was an adjustment for coach Kori Cheverie, who wouldn't have the opportunity to have another practice with her team again between the Battle on Bay Street and the team's next game back home against Minnesota. "Sometimes I can't even keep up with everything that's going on, we're moving so fast," Cheverie had said before the Toronto game. "[I'm] definitely learning about all of the different aspects that it takes to run a team, how much we can be involved or how much we don't need to be involved. Sometimes as a coach, I want to know absolutely everything. I think if I tried to know everything, I'd drive myself crazy. It's really just trying to make sure that things are running smoothly, making sure our athletes are getting the right type of exposure but also being able to stay rested as much as possible, too."

One of the decisions the team had to make was to decide what to do with Catherine Dubois, who was nearing the end of a second ten-day contract. She wouldn't be able to play again during the regular season unless she signed a full contract. No one could deny that Dubois's game fit the PWHL's style of play well, but someone else would need to move off the roster for that to happen. While it was up to Cheverie, the coach, to decide whether Dubois would be in the lineup and what kind of role she would play, the question of whether and how she could be signed fell to Danièle Sauvageau, the manager.

January had been an emotional month for Dubois, who never knew what each day might bring. Would she be in the next lineup? Would this be her last game in a Montréal jersey? She doubted herself and whether she belonged in the league. To add to the uncertainty, Dubois had been the first reserve player activated in the brand-new league. Everyone was still feeling out how everything worked, and Dubois was the first to test everything. But she kept pushing on, kept working hard, and hoping that maybe, one day, she would make it to the roster full time.

The day after the Battle on Bay Street, and the day before the Minnesota game, Dubois got a call from Sauvageau. The team offered Dubois a contract for the rest of the season. Defender Dominika Lásková was hurt at the end of January and moved to the long-term injured reserve, which opened up one of Montréal's twenty-three contract spots. The team didn't say it publicly at the time, but Lásková would need surgery. She was done for the season and wouldn't play a game again for more than a year. It was a huge blow for her.

But in sports, one person's misfortune is sometimes another person's lifeline. When Sauvageau gave Dubois the news, Dubois cried. Sauvageau also told her she'd be playing in Montréal's game the next day at home against Minnesota. Dubois called her family, and they cried together. The fact that her pro hockey dream came true so close to home made it more special. Dubois's grandmother watched her play for the first time in fifteen years, and now her family would have more opportunities to see her live out her dream.

Cheverie had been vague with reporters who'd been asking about Dubois's future at every media availability leading up to this moment. Now, she could say it was a no brainer to sign Dubois. "What she brings to the lineup is something that I think every team wishes they had—someone who is fearless, will go into corners, will get pucks, and will stand in front of the net," the coach said after the Dubois contract was announced. "That's what she brings on the ice. But off the ice, everybody loves her in the dressing room. She's definitely a fan favourite among our group."

Dubois's family made last-minute plans to head from Quebec City to Laval the next day for the game against Minnesota. The team had drawn more than six thousand fans to Place Bell at its first home game and more than eight thousand at the second. This Sunday afternoon game was the first time the team sold out Place Bell. The game, dubbed Minor Hockey Day, officially drew 10,172 fans, including many kids who wore their hockey jerseys. Some of the PWHL players also wore their minor hockey jerseys, too, as they walked into the rink. Before the game began, a long lineup of people wanting to buy merchandise snaked through the concourse.

Montréal won the game 2–1, earning the valuable three points awarded for a regulation win. It was backup goaltender Elaine Chuli's fourth win in four starts, proving she was a solid option alongside Desbiens. Montréal gave up twenty-two shots, far fewer than in the last three games, when the team had yielded a total of ninety-five shots. Most importantly, the team finally broke through on its power-play drought thanks to a goal from rookie Claire Dalton, who had earned Cheverie's trust by being a versatile player who could confidently fit anywhere in the lineup. Cheverie, who typically started her post-game press conferences with a statement in French, had a short and sweet one on this day. "Enfin, l'avantage numérique," she said—finally, the power play. Reporters, she suggested, could start asking her about a different topic.

While it was a relief to see the team finally score a power-play goal, Cheverie had known all along it was coming. The team's plan that night had been for players to shoot from the middle of the ice, no matter the situation. Sure enough, after defender Kati Tabin spent some extra time to find a lane in the middle of the ice to shoot, Dalton got a stick on the puck in front. "We have the personnel to do it," Cheverie said about scoring on the power play. "Honestly, the power play is simple. It's about doing the most simple things correct over and over again. It's not a special play. It's about numbers at the net, it's about getting shots through, and it's about outnumbering them."

As Cheverie mixed up the lines, Dubois also spent some time on the first line with Marie-Philip Poulin, a good way for Dubois to start her stint on a full contract. Cheverie knew what she was getting when she put Dubois on that top line. Dubois was predictable in a good way. You knew she would go hard, not be scared, and dig pucks out of corners. Cheverie thought that would create a bit of space for Poulin on the top line and for Poulin's typical linemates, Maureen Murphy and Tereza Vanišová, who had been drawing the hardest matchups alongside Poulin. "She usually steps up," Cheverie said about Dubois. "She doesn't have time to think about it, because I do it on the fly. She just has to get out there."

With a contract in hand, Dubois finally had some stability. Most of all, she felt grateful for the opportunity and the people around her who'd made it possible, from her university coach, Isabelle Leclaire, who changed how she thought about herself, to the friend who let her stay in her apartment while she chased her hockey dreams. “I don’t understand why I’m so lucky in life, to be honest,” Dubois said in an interview a few weeks later. “If I wasn’t that well surrounded, there’s no way I could play hockey this year. There’s no way you can do that by yourself. No chance.”

13
A PERSON FIRST, A HOCKEY PLAYER SECOND

March 10, 2024
Laval, Quebec

Montréal rattled off three wins in a row to end February and begin March. The streak stopped with another matchup against Toronto that ended in a loss to the rival team, with Toronto again shutting Montréal out. It was a physical game where, at one point, six players were sent off for roughing after tempers flared. When a fourth player joined Montréal's penalty box, it was so crowded that everyone had to stand.

An even bigger loss came in the game against Toronto: Marie-Philip Poulin sustained an injury that caused her to miss the rest of March. Not only was Poulin a key part of Montréal's offence, but she was also one of the best defensive players on the team. At the end of the loss against Toronto, even as she seemed to be labouring, Poulin chased down Toronto's Sarah Nurse, who was barrelling toward an empty net. She broke up the play and kept her team alive a little longer. Poulin was known for her big goals at clutch moments, but she was just as valuable to the team for her willingness to block a shot or make a big hit.

Poulin's injury came in the midst of what had been a gruelling early March. Within the first ten days, the team had played games in Montréal, Connecticut, Toronto, and back home again. The intensely physical games and relentless schedule seemed to be taking its toll. After the last game in that marathon, a 4–2 loss at home against Ottawa, Laura Stacey wore the fatigue on her face. She said her own play fell short that night, that she could have done some little things better that might have changed the outcome, especially with Poulin out of the lineup. "All of you guys know exactly the impact she can have, and we know that, too, so we tried our best to kind of fill that void, fill that hole and work together as a team," Stacey told reporters after the game. "Obviously, we came up short. But we're going to put our heads back down, get back to work, and try to figure it out for the next one."

After that game, players got a rare break in the schedule with a few days of precious practice time. That meant head coach Kori Cheverie's night wasn't done after the game ended. She spent the next couple of hours making a game plan for how to best use the days ahead. That was something Cheverie could control. When her captain might be back was out of her hands. She described her star player's injury as day to day. *Day to day* is one of those hockey terms that tells you a lot without really telling you much at all. It means the injury isn't serious enough to end a player's season, but it could also mean tomorrow or next week or longer than that. Months have a lot of days in them. "I'm not confident and I'm not *not* confident," Cheverie said when reporters asked about Poulin's status for the next game. "I'm kind of in the middle, and I try to stay as even-keel as I can, because I don't know right now. I don't know when that is. We're doing what we've done with all of our players all year: we're making sure that they're healthy and their health is the number-one priority."

When the team was back in Verdun to practise a couple days later, they had to share the arena with figure skaters preparing for the world championship in Montréal. As the skaters dangled from ropes hung from the arena ceiling, practising acrobatics and jumps to instrumental music, the PWHL players worked away in the building's smaller rink. Poulin wasn't on the ice that day, and Georges Flahiff noticed. The eighty-year-old was a fixture on Verdun's wooden benches when the team was on the ice. On those days, he would board the train at the Atwater station near his home, travelling twenty minutes each way to the rink. He'd been following women's hockey in the city for decades, through leagues gone by and finally to the PWHL, where the crowds were growing bigger than he'd seen before. When he first saw a teenaged Poulin play for the CWHL's Montréal Stars, he knew she'd be a superstar. But over the years, what he'd come to love most about Poulin was her kindness to others at the rink, including him. Earlier that season, Poulin and Stacey had both given him autographed sticks.

On this day, he watched the practice from a bench that faced a window looking into the smaller rink, a spot where you can stay warm and still see all the action. He flagged a passing reporter down and urged her to ask: when will Poulin return to play?

For Montréal fans, it was the most important question to answer, one that Montréal's season might depend on.

The practice days back in Montréal were a break from the travel, but the team was still busy.

One day in mid-March, defender Erin Ambrose rose at seven thirty, drank her morning coffee, and took her dog, Henry, for a walk through the streets of Montréal. Then it was off to Verdun Auditorium for breakfast with the team, followed by a video meeting, a lifting session, and on-ice practice. On this day, Ambrose also had a photoshoot with CCM and LGBTQ+ advocate Brock McGillis as part of a pride-themed merchandise line she designed. The proceeds went to McGillis's

Alphabet Sports Collective, a non-profit that works to make hockey more inclusive and accepting for people from all sexualities and gender expressions. That advocacy, along with her openness about her mental health, was something Ambrose always made time for.

In between her commitments that day, she sat down with a reporter on a bench looking into the rink to reflect on what had so far been a grind of a season. Ambrose was playing huge minutes for Montréal in all situations. She averaged more ice time in February than any other player in the league. What she brought to the table took on even more importance with defender Dominika Lásková out with an injury. Sometimes she didn't know her tank was running low until it was empty. That's where she found herself in mid-February after weeks of travel with Montréal, national-team commitments, and the emotional highs of so many big moments. "I think it was a combination of everything, of just not taking care of myself," Ambrose said. Even though it was still busy, being at home for a stretch was an opportunity to reset.

The last time Ambrose had a comparable schedule over a full season might have been in college at Clarkson University. Ambrose struggled significantly in those years and had blacked out some parts of it in her mind. But now she pushed herself to try to remember how she had dealt with such a demanding schedule. When hockey became all consuming, it was easy to lose herself in the sport, prioritizing Erin the hockey player and forgetting about Erin the person. What worked for another player might not be what she needed. She had to figure out what worked for her to help herself adjust to the new league.

One tool she turned to was scheduling more frequent appointments with her psychiatrist. Poulin and Stacey, two of Ambrose's best friends, also helped her navigate things. Being around them, even doing something as simple as having dinner together or hanging out in Ambrose's hotel room after a game, gave her a lot of joy. So did

Erin Ambrose, left, in a Montréal jersey, battles league MVP and Toronto forward Natalie Spooner in front of Ann-Renée Desbiens at the net during a game in the PWHL's first season; Ambrose played big minutes for the team throughout that year.
(Ellen Bond Photo)

walks with Henry, which allowed her to forget whatever might have been going on at the rink. But perhaps the biggest way Ambrose got through a busy season was by talking to her sister and infant nephew on video calls, sometimes as often as four times a day. Her sister always listened and so did her nephew, even if he might not have understood everything she was saying yet. "I talk to him constantly," Ambrose said. "I can tell him whatever I want."

After getting cut from the Olympic team in 2018, Ambrose had become disconnected from her family, feeling like she'd let them down. It was uncharacteristic and a major red flag in a family that's normally so close. Now, the frequent calls with her nephew helped to keep her connection to her family strong and gave her a reason to reach out every day, to keep her most important ties strong. Her darkest days had taught her an important lesson: you don't need to be 100 per cent in on hockey all the time. "I can have things away from the ice that make me happy. That's going to lead to me being a happier person and being a better hockey player," Ambrose said. Even though she was one of the team's most important players, and the anchor on the back end, the people in Ambrose's corner, her nephew included, didn't care how she performed on the ice. To them, she was just Erin.

Amanda Boulier was holding her newborn niece for the first time when a text appeared on her phone. It was from Ottawa general manager Mike Hirshfeld, who asked if the defender had a couple of minutes to chat. It was March 18, 2024, the league's first trade deadline day. Boulier was visiting her family in Connecticut, where her Ottawa team was set to play a game against New York in two days. But it now felt unlikely that she'd play in that game.

"I think you're going to have to hold her, because I think I'm about to be traded," the defender told her brother.

Her suspicions were right: Boulier was heading to Montréal. Montréal had needed a right-shooting, top-four defender now that Dominika Lásková was injured, someone who could take some of the load off Erin Ambrose and Kati Tabin. Forward Tereza Vanišová was going the other way to Ottawa. Although the trade would separate Vanišová from her best friend Lásková, a few familiar faces were in Ottawa. The head coach, Carla MacLeod, had coached Vanišová on the Czechia team, and two Czech teammates played in Ottawa, too.

For most female hockey players, the prospect of being traded without having a say in the matter had never really been a possibility.

Where players competed often had a lot to do with where they had other jobs and family ties. It wasn't realistic to ask someone to move elsewhere when they made little to nothing to play hockey. The PWHL's collective bargaining agreement allowed trades, with some protection for players, including a requirement to cover moving costs. The idea became reality a few weeks before Boulier was moved, when Minnesota and Boston connected on the league's first trade. Boston sent rookie defender Sophie Jaques, who'd had a slow start, to Minnesota in exchange for Finnish forward Susanna Tapani, hoping she could jumpstart an anemic offence. Boston also got depth defender Abby Cook in the trade. It was a reminder to players that trades could happen at any time in this new league.

For Boulier, a trade hadn't been on her radar. She said players felt like there probably wouldn't be much movement at the deadline, especially since teams couldn't trade draft picks in the first season. Instead, three trades occurred, including the one Boulier was involved in. It came as a bit of a surprise. "As a professional athlete, it kind of always has to be in the back of your mind, which I think it was but probably not as much as it maybe should have been," Boulier said in an interview a few weeks after the trade to Montréal. She was sad to leave the people in Ottawa, but she felt no resentment about the trade. At the very least, she got the news while she was with her family. "We wanted a professional league," she said, "and this is just a product of that."

Quebec would be the fourth province or state where Boulier had lived over the span of a year, and the next step in a playing career that had almost ended a couple of times. Boulier grew up looking up to her two older brothers. They played hockey, so she wanted to play, too. She was only two years old when she watched their games at the rink and begged to be allowed on the ice. One time, she even showed up to the rink in a neck guard.

When she turned three, her parents let her play. Beyond wanting to follow her brothers, Boulier loved the speed and technique of skating. She loved the dynamics of a team and how much could happen in a forty-five-second shift. The sport felt unique to her, different from any other. Boulier played Division I hockey at St. Lawrence University in New York state. When she finished her college career in 2016, professional female hockey player didn't feel like a viable career path. She felt the only way to stay in the game would be to coach, so she accepted a job at Yale University. But after a year away from playing, she heard the Connecticut Whale of the NWHL/PHF was looking for an extra defender. She offered to fill in when her coaching schedule at Yale allowed it. "That was a blessing and a curse as soon as I started playing again," Boulier said. "I was like, oh boy, I think I have to stop coaching because I love playing so much."

Being both a player and a coach had its benefits. She could relate to players better as a coach because she had a player's perspective. As a player, she saw the game from a whole new vantage point by stepping back and really letting herself be a student of the game and learning it inside out as a coach. She ultimately left her job at Yale and spent the next five seasons playing in the PHF, winning championships with both the Minnesota Whitecaps and Boston Pride teams. Her playing career was in flux again in the summer of 2023 when the PHF folded. Boulier was at a restaurant with friends when rumblings of the league-wide call reached her. Then, she was at home with her parents and fiancée when she found out the league was no more. There was shock and sadness as people worked out the logistics. "It was also just a really exciting time once you were able to kind of process the news for the sport," Boulier recalled. "I would say initial sadness, but then you kind of see the big picture and you realize that the sport needed one league."

Still, Boulier's own career was unclear. She'd turned thirty a few months earlier and had no idea what kind of direction the league might go in and whether there might be a spot for her. She took a week away from hockey to decide whether she wanted to keep playing. Ultimately, she decided she wanted to try and continued training and skating. Around the same time, Boulier's fiancée got a job coaching hockey in Boston, and they moved from Minnesota. A few months later, Boulier would move to Ottawa, the team that drafted her in the thirteenth round.

And then, three months into the season, she was on the move again. After the trade, Boulier caught a flight back to Ottawa that landed at nine p.m. She had to pack up her apartment and get to Montréal for a nine o'clock practice the next morning. As she packed, she approached it as a new adventure. Sleep would come another day, and so would settling in. She just had to get it done and move forward. The drive to Montréal took about three hours. Boulier allowed herself to be sad for the first forty-five minutes to an hour, to reminisce about the teammates she was leaving. Then she turned the page. She told herself that players didn't have time to be sad. They had to go to practice, and they had to perform. She was a professional athlete, paid to play hockey, and had to put her emotions aside.

When she arrived in Montréal, meeting all the players and staff was a whirlwind. Everyone was welcoming and excited for her to join the team. The day passed in a blur, and that night she crashed in her hotel room. She didn't get much time to settle in because a couple of days later, the team was off to Minnesota for its last game before the league paused for three weeks for the world championship. But the former coach knew early on that she'd found the right place with head coach Kori Cheverie and her staff. "Kori is such an elite hockey mind," Boulier said. The first day she was given access to the team's chat, she was impressed with the level of detail Cheverie uses in her coaching and systems. It was immediately clear to Boulier that Cheverie understands and thinks about the game at a high level. In Boulier, Montréal got a player that Ottawa's GM credited with helping create his team's culture and who he described as one of the nicest and funniest people he's met in hockey. On the ice, the team finally had more depth on defence. Boulier could be the number two defender on the right side behind Ambrose.

With forwards Kennedy Marchment and Ann-Sophie Bettez out with long-term injuries and Poulin still out, too, the team also added a forward, free agent Mikyla Grant-Mentis. Grant-Mentis had racked up points in the PHF en route to the MVP award in 2021, an achievement that earned her an $80,000 deal with the league's Buffalo Beauts. Not all salaries in that league were public, but she was believed to be the highest-paid player at the time. But when the PWHL held its draft, no team picked Grant-Mentis. She signed as a free agent with Ottawa and then was released in February, despite recording three assists in six games. Montréal, however, spotted opportunity in Grant-Mentis. In Montréal's first game of the season against Ottawa, Cheverie saw a player who could be a difference maker, one with the ability to find open ice and create space for her teammates. She believed that in the right environment, Grant-Mentis could thrive. She joined the team before a trip to play a neutral-site game in Pittsburgh, eager to show what she could do. In addition to Grant-Mentis, the team could also call on Olympic gold medallist Mélodie Daoust, who wasn't available to play with the team full time and was a member of the reserve list. Named the tournament MVP at the 2018 Olympics, Daoust had scored a goal in her PWHL debut in March and was eligible to sign one more ten-day contract in the regular season.

Despite the new additions, however, the team still struggled offensively without Poulin. They endured another loss to Toronto, 2–1, followed by a 3–2 shootout loss in Minnesota. In the Minnesota game, Montréal came out strong with two early goals but let the lead slip away. Cheverie made it clear that she wanted to see more of a killer instinct from her team. She got that at the beginning of the game, but she didn't like how they responded when Minnesota came back. A bright spot was Boulier's play. Despite Boulier's whirlwind week, Cheverie liked her quick decision-making and how fast she got to pucks. But the losses meant Montréal went into the three-week break having lost four in a row, its worst stretch all season. "We continue to build and we continue to put our process in place," Cheverie said after the Minnesota loss. "I've liked what we've seen from our team over the past few games. We just haven't been able to score more than the other team. That's really the long and the short of it."

There was some bright news in the middle of it. After weeks of rumours, the league confirmed that Montréal and Toronto would play a game at the Bell Centre on April 20. It was dubbed the Duel at the Top, a nod to the fact that both teams were still jockeying for placement atop the standings. When the tickets went on sale at the end of March, they sold out in minutes, all but ensuring Montréal would break the attendance record set at Scotiabank Arena in Toronto earlier in the season.

The next few weeks held more uncharted territory. The national-team players would head to Utica, New York, to compete in the world championship in the middle of their PWHL season. Cheverie was also going as an assistant coach with Team Canada. The rest of the players and staff would spend most of the break back in Montréal practising. For some PWHL teams, the break was a momentum killer. But for a Montréal team that had just lost four games, the break would be the reset the team needed.

14
SHE'S GAY, MARCUS

April 18, 2024
Montréal, Quebec

The sound at Verdun Auditorium increased another decibel when Montréal captain Marie-Philip Poulin was announced as a member of the team's starting lineup. More than a month had passed since Poulin last skated out in a Montréal jersey. She'd finished March on the injured list but made a comeback in April to lead Team Canada to a world championship, the fourth of her career. In addition to Poulin, players Erin Ambrose, Laura Stacey, Ann-Renée Desbiens, and Kristin O'Neill, and coach Kori Cheverie returned with gold medals and an extra spring in their step from the experience.

They had to quickly shift gears back into PWHL mode. Each team had five games left in the regular season before playoffs were set to begin. Montréal had limped into the break on a four-game losing streak but still held a grip on a playoff spot in third place, four points behind second-place Minnesota and four points ahead of fourth-place Ottawa. With three points for a regulation win, a lot of things could shift in the final stretch.

Minnesota was the visitor on this night, and that team had lots to play for. A regulation win over Montréal could clinch Minnesota a playoff spot. Montréal, meanwhile, was celebrating Pride Night at Verdun.

When Stacey had scored the game-tying goal in Montréal's first game against Ottawa back on January 2, Toronto hockey journalist Omar White tweeted a GIF of the moment. "Score a goal and celly with your fiance," he wrote. Another account, by the name of MarcusA9393, responded: "Her fiancee is there? Didn't see him behind the glass." Poulin and Stacey were engaged to each other, and it wasn't immediately clear if Marcus truly didn't know that or was trying to make trouble. "Her fiancée is #29 Poulin," 22JQuinn responded. "She's gay, Marcus."

The whole sequence went viral, mimicking the moment a couple years earlier when someone on social media mistook soccer stars Kristie Mewis and Sam Kerr as great friends, only to be told, "They're lesbians, Stacey." People took screenshots of the "She's gay, Marcus" tweet alongside the photo of Poulin and Stacey embracing, towering over Ottawa forward Becca Gilmore's skates, as she sprawled on the ice beside them. "She's gay, Marcus" became the first PWHL meme, finding its way onto signs, T-shirts, and friendship bracelets at games for the rest of the season. It was about more than Poulin and Stacey and their relationship. It was an early sign the league would be welcoming, and that people who haven't always seen themselves reflected in the sport could find a home in the PWHL.

That fall, the NHL had ended the practice of teams wearing jerseys for special causes after several players refused to wear pride jerseys. At first, that ban also extended to using multicoloured pride tape on sticks. That decision drew criticism from the head of the PWHL Players Association, Brian Burke, who has been a staunch advocate for 2SLGBTQIA+ inclusion in the sport. Burke and his son Patrick co-created the You Can Play campaign to rid sports of homophobia following the death of Brendan Burke, Burke's second son and Patrick's younger brother, in a car accident in 2010. A former hockey player who was the student manager with the Miami University men's hockey team, Brendan was one of the first high-profile men in hockey to come out publicly when he did so in 2009, and he became a leading voice and advocate for making the sport a more welcoming place for people in the 2SLGBTQIA+ community. Fifteen years after Brendan came out, the NHL still hasn't had an openly gay player.

By banning pride tape, Burke argued, the league was taking away the opportunity for teams and players to support a number of different important causes. "Let's be clear: this is not inclusion or progress," Burke wrote on social media. "This does not grow the game, and does not make our fans feel welcome." The PWHL is home to a significant number of players who are part of the 2SLGBTQIA+ community, and the players' association put out a statement saying the NHL's decision "sets back years of progress." The NHL ultimately reversed the ban, after Arizona Coyotes defenceman Travis Dermott defied it and used rainbow tape on his stick anyway. The episode was a reminder that, no matter how many times it's written in a press release, hockey doesn't always feel like it's for everyone.

But women's hockey has always been a bit different. While the sport has a long way to go to become more racially diverse and accessible to all, it has always been home to women who present in different ways. Some women are more masculine and some are more feminine, some are straight and others are not, and they co-exist in the same locker room. That has created a fundamentally different culture than the one built into men's hockey, according to Kristi Allain, a sociologist at St. Thomas University in Fredericton who has studied masculinity in hockey. "Part of the protective feature of women's hockey that helps save it from some of the tragic consequences of men's hockey culture is that there is a real diversity of gender expression," Allain explained. Even with that diversity, female hockey players have not always felt comfortable being open publicly about their sexuality, whether it's because they didn't want to be treated differently, because of the way society perceives women who present in a more masculine way, or simply because they wanted to keep their personal lives private. But that has been changing. Players like Erin Ambrose and Jamie Lee Rattray, to name just two, advocate for the 2SLGBTQIA+ community. Having two faces of the league in Poulin and Stacey be open about their relationship is significant representation that people in the community haven't always had growing up.

It meant a lot to them, too. At first, watching "She's gay, Marcus" blow up the way it did after their first game together was a bit much for Poulin and Stacey. Their play on the ice has nothing to do with their off-ice relationship, and they're private people. Eventually, they embraced it. They wore T-shirts emblazoned with the photo and the viral post at their bachelorette party months later. Everyone else wore "She's gay, Marcus" bracelets. "I honestly think that it's amazing to see the way this league, this sport, has come around and supported every single one of us, the two of us especially," Stacey said in a video posted on the PWHL Montréal Instagram account a few months after the infamous goal. "Just to allow everybody the opportunity to feel like they can play, that they can be there, that they can be supported, I think this picture says a lot."

Poulin would later tell Devin Heroux from CBC Sports that she was the most herself she'd ever been in that first PWHL season. Poulin was finally able to play in a league again, leading a team in her home province, free from having to face questions about league building. She could just play hockey, the thing she does better than just about anyone on the planet, something she enjoys so much that you'll often find a smiley face drawn on the tape at the top of her stick. That season was also the most she'd shared with the world about who she is as a person. She wasn't just a hockey player who scored big goals at big moments for her country. She was a friend to her teammates, the one often cracking jokes—a personality she seemed to feel more comfortable than ever sharing with the public. She was also a partner to Stacey and became her wife in a ceremony in the summer of 2024. Their relationship was out there in the world, a part of her she'd never shared publicly before.

Journalist Jared Book covered Poulin for years in the CWHL and after the league folded. She seemed different to him in the PWHL's first season. She was more at ease, more comfortable. Book always felt Poulin knew she had to be in the spotlight because of who she was as a player, but that she never really enjoyed it, partly because she has always been shy. Now, she was having fun with it, even if she still shied away from the spotlight or praise. She embraced her role as a face of the game, and people embraced Poulin, every part of her, fully.

That was obvious across the rink in Verdun on Pride Night in April, with references to Poulin and Stacey, and the infamous Marcus, on many fans' signs. The team even brought in artist Samantha Woj to paint the iconic "She's gay, Marcus" photo of Poulin and Stacey using only a hockey puck. The crowd waved colourful thundersticks and pride and trans-pride flags, and many of the players taped their sticks with rainbow-coloured pride tape.

A few minutes into the game, when Minnesota's Brittyn Fleming was called for delay of game, Montréal's top power-play unit took the ice. Kristin O'Neill had moved up to the first power-play unit in March, amid Poulin's absence and the Tereza Vanišová trade. With Poulin back, Montréal debuted a new unit that featured Poulin, O'Neill, Stacey, Ambrose, and Maureen Murphy. O'Neill had been named one of Team Canada's top players at the world championship and had made it a goal to bring that confidence back to Montréal with her. After struggling on the power play all season—Montréal entered the game with an 8.1 per cent efficiency rate, the second worst in the league—something clicked: O'Neill put in her own rebound at the side of the net for her second goal of the season. Then it happened again, this time on a shot by Poulin during a power play toward the end of the first period. The movement of the players on the power play made it so hard for Minnesota to defend that Poulin found herself open in front of the Minnesota goaltender for a second. That's all the time Poulin needed.

After the momentum of the first, Montréal let Minnesota creep back in the game, giving up three back-to-back goals in the second period. But everyone on Montréal knew how March had ended, and they didn't want to lose five in a row. The team went into the home stretch treating the final five games as a brand-new season. During a TV timeout in the third period, coach Kori Cheverie talked to goaltender Elaine Chuli about exactly when to leave the ice for an extra attacker. With Montréal still trailing by a goal late in the third period, Cheverie took a risk. With nearly three minutes left in the game, she decided to pull Chuli. It's easy to second guess when to pull your goaltender, and it did feel a bit early. But Cheverie knew if they could get the momentum early enough in the third, they could still pull off a regulation win.

With the extra attacker on the ice, the puck came back toward the blue line to Ambrose. She passed it up to Stacey, who fired a one-timer over the Minnesota goaltender. When she saw the puck go in, Stacey threw her arms in the air and then bent her knees down low in what felt like her biggest goal celebration of the season to date. Tie game. Less than two minutes remained on the clock when Minnesota's Maggie Flaherty went off for holding, giving Montréal a golden opportunity to pull ahead. With forty-seven seconds left, O'Neill scored her second goal of the game, and her first game-winning goal of the season. Verdun Auditorium erupted. Montréal's 4–3 win completed the comeback in regulation, earned the team a valuable three points, and robbed Minnesota of the opportunity to clinch a playoff spot. Ambrose finished with assists on all four goals. She became the first player in the PWHL to record four points in a single game, all four passes coming off her stick wrapped in rainbow-coloured tape on a night that was hugely important to her as a proud member of the 2SLGBTQIA+ community. The rink felt electric after the win, all the doom and gloom of March clearly behind this team. "It feels like a long time ago," Cheverie said that night about her team's difficult March. "I feel like I've lived three lives this season."

While O'Neill had contributed on the ice defensively, the puck hadn't been going into the net for her at the beginning of the season. Now the dam had broken. It was a continuation of momentum she'd started to build at the world championship, something she credited to a mindset shift. Playing on a line with two college players at worlds gave her a fresh perspective, she said. The line felt they could play as themselves and had a lot of success as a result. Her Montréal teammates on Team Canada encouraged her to believe she could bring that confidence back to the PWHL.

Sitting beside O'Neill in the media room after the game, Poulin told reporters that she knew O'Neill's hard work would pay off on the scoresheet. O'Neill is the type of player who does things right on and off the ice, who holds herself accountable and makes her teammates better every day, the captain said. "When you play with the heart and details, day in and day out, it's a matter of time," Poulin said.

The win drew Montréal closer to the top of the standings, putting the team just one point behind second-place Minnesota. First-place Toronto, which lost that night, was also in reach. Only two points separated the team from Montréal. The teams faced some extra incentive to finish first. Earlier, the league had announced that four of the six teams would make the playoffs, and that the first-place team would get to choose its opponent between the third- and fourth-place teams.

Inside the media room, a reporter asked Cheverie if she knew that Toronto had lost that night. "I heard that. That's nice—for us," she said with a smile. "Statistically speaking. It's just factual." Cheverie seemed to grow more comfortable with the crowd of media as the season went on, even joking with reporters that night that she practised French by watching the Quebecois version of her favourite show, *Survivor*. During the world championship, she conducted an interview with RDS in French, something that would have been unthinkable before the season. It added another layer to her job but one she embraced. Every game, she had to think of a game plan for the team on the ice, and she also had to think about what she might say in French that day. But spending time studying French with her teacher was also a break from thinking about hockey.

Her whole life, Cheverie has tried to put herself in situations that will make her grow. Learning French as the first-time head coach of a team in a brand-new league with a giant media following was just one example. "The feedback that I've received, it's encouraging," she said of her efforts to learn French. "That's something that I want to continue, and I want to continue to get great at it."

The win gave Montréal the momentum it needed to ride into the next game at the Bell Centre. The energy from the more than three thousand fans at Verdun Auditorium felt electric. But the team couldn't prepare for what a crowd of more than twenty-one thousand would feel like.

15
THE DUEL AT THE TOP

April 19, 2024
Montréal, Quebec

The day after the emotional win over Minnesota, PWHL Montréal's leaders lined up at a table inside a media room in the bowels of the Bell Centre: captain Marie-Philip Poulin, assistant captain Laura Stacey, starting goaltender Ann-Renée Desbiens, general manager Danièle Sauvageau, and head coach Kori Cheverie. The team didn't usually hold a formal press conference the day before playing a game, but this wasn't just any game. This was the day before twenty-one thousand people would celebrate women's hockey in a building that means an enormous amount to hockey in Montréal. Growing up in Quebec meant watching the Canadiens and being aware of how many Stanley Cups the team had won in its long history, Desbiens said. "I think it's our turn now to have the torch and hold it high and be proud of everything that's been done for women's hockey. For us to be able to have this platform tomorrow, I'm sure we're going to take advantage of it. We're going to do [our] best, and we're going to enjoy every single moment of it."

It wasn't the first time the Bell Centre had hosted a professional women's hockey game. In December 2016, nearly six thousand fans, a really good turnout for the CWHL, watched Les Canadiennes defeat the Calgary Inferno in the Bell Centre. Almost a year later, Poulin played here with Les Canadiennes again. She'd looked up at the empty seats in the lower bowl and beyond and hoped that someday they would be packed for women's hockey. She couldn't have imagined that, more than six years later and several years after that team and league folded, she'd be sitting here, about to play in front of a sold-out Bell Centre crowd. The same sport that drew only a few thousand to the Bell Centre six years earlier had sold out this arena in minutes this time around.

Perhaps the most unbelievable part, for people who have followed women's hockey for years, is not just that it sold out, but that selling out was the expectation. Even before this game was announced, Montréal players talked about how they wanted to break the attendance record set in Toronto in February. Montréal holding the record was a point of pride for them.

Jayna Hefford is conservative by nature, probably a good quality in a senior vice-president of hockey operations. Everyone was talking about breaking a record, but what if they sold only fifteen thousand tickets? That would still be a big success. She measured her expectations. Sure enough, she was wrong. They could have sold even more tickets if the Bell Centre held more seats. At events around town, Sauvageau fielded questions about how to get tickets to the game.

You could call it a dream come true, but as Stacey described it, it's beyond what the players could have ever dreamed about. "I think when we were all young kids, we saw the Olympics on TV," Stacey said at the press conference. "We wanted to play for Team Canada. We saw the packed buildings that Team Canada got to play in. We wanted to wear that gold medal and hear our national anthem. But we never thought that playing professionally in a place like the Bell Centre was ever a dream or a possibility."

Laura Stacey, Kori Cheverie, Danièle Sauvageau, Marie-Philip Poulin, and Ann-Renée Desbiens at a special press conference at the Bell Centre, the day before the team's big game in the arena. (Karissa Donkin)

Nor did Cheverie, not when she was growing up in Nova Scotia and not when she was playing in the CWHL herself. Like Stacey, Poulin, and Desbiens, she also dreamed of playing on the Olympic team because that's where she saw women playing. Like so many, she didn't make the Olympic team as a player. But she's gotten to experience these moments as a coach, still one of few women coaching hockey professionally. Looking at the state of professional women's hockey when she finished her career in 2016—before she turned thirty, because she couldn't turn down an opportunity to move into coaching when playing didn't pay—she could see how far it had come in less than a decade. "The opportunity that [players] had four or five years ago to make a stance and decide that they deserved something better, and they were going to put the work in until something better came about—that's how change happens," the coach said.

It certainly isn't something Sauvageau could have dreamed about as a girl, when she wasn't even allowed to play with the boys in organized hockey. Maybe on the pond in Deux-Montagnes she could dream about playing for the Montréal Canadiens, about the crowd chanting her name. But to be a star in a women's hockey league and sell out the Bell Centre? Unimaginable. And yet she saw the potential when she built Centre 21.02 before the league even existed. She saw it again when the league began, and she worked behind the scenes with the Montréal Canadiens to make this game happen.

This game was also one last chance to slay PWHL Montréal's Toronto demons by beating the team that had had their number all season long. And as the Duel at the Top name suggested, it was a chance to move up in the standings. Every point mattered.

It wasn't lost on Stacey that so many women, Sauvageau and Cheverie included, never got an opportunity to play in the spotlight of a big stage like the Bell Centre. That her own career lined up with the time this league started felt lucky to her. She also thought of the kids who would now be able to dream of this very moment. That future generation is never far from Poulin's mind, either. She's always the player they want to meet, the one they look up to, and she always makes time for them. Poulin struggled to put into words what it would feel like to skate onto the ice. "There are so many great players who've been here before us," the captain said. "In terms of women's hockey, being able to fill that ice tomorrow, it's going to be surreal."

—

The anticipation buzzed inside the Bell Centre long before the players skated on to the ice. When the crowd caught a glimpse of them, the noise reached ninety decibels.

But the loudest cheers of all came when Marie-Philip Poulin was introduced on the blue line. It felt like a thank you for all she's meant to the sport, an appreciation for how long she'd waited for this day, and how long the women before her had waited for a day that, for them, never came. It felt overdue, and as reporter Jared Book pointed out, the Bell Centre crowd is known for lengthy ovations. They might still be cheering for Poulin inside the Bell Centre to this day if Ann-Renée Desbiens hadn't been next in line to be introduced.

The 21,105-person crowd set a world record for the best-attended women's hockey game, and they sounded even more than 21,105 strong. They cheered every possession, shot, and block so loudly that Kori Cheverie's ears rang, and Erin Ambrose's teammates struggled to hear her. During play stoppages, Ambrose scanned the crowd, taking it all in, feeling how each person wanted to fire her team up. Forward Sarah Bujold felt speechless when she heard the crowd during the game. It made her a little emotional. *This is crazy*, she thought. *They're cheering for* us.

A Montréal goal in front of the home crowd might have blown the roof off, but Toronto struck first. Toronto captain Blayre Turnbull got her team on the board nine and a half minutes into the first period. The moment more than twenty-one thousand people were waiting for came toward the end of the first period. Bujold evened the score, and the stands erupted.

For Bujold, the moment felt hard to believe. Bujold had watched her contract disappear the previous summer when the PHF shut down.

She practised for months in New Brunswick, getting ice where she could and not knowing if she'd have a job when the new league started. She didn't hear her name called at September's draft. But Bujold found a home in Montréal, and she got to experience more than twenty-one thousand fans applauding her. As she headed back to the bench, she couldn't wipe the smile off her face. Teammate Maureen Murphy made a heart symbol over Bujold's head for the camera. It ended up being Bujold's final game in a Montréal sweater. An injury cost her the rest of the season. But it was a game and a goal she will remember for the rest of her life.

Toronto and Montréal traded goals again in the second: one from Toronto's Sarah Nurse, and one from Montréal's Ambrose. The latter came on Montréal's red-hot power play. The score remained tied as regulation time ran out. Unfortunately for the Montréal fans, it took only thirteen seconds for Nurse to score the overtime game winner. This might have been Montréal's best performance against league-leading Toronto, but for the fifth and final time in the league's inaugural season, Toronto beat Montréal. Toronto secured a playoff spot with the win, and Montréal would have to try again the next game.

Cheverie told reporters later that her team is usually pretty quiet after a loss. But this game felt different. There were positives to take from their performance as they went into the home stretch. Beyond the final score, it felt hard to shake the excitement of a sold-out Bell Centre crowd, plus the moment of admiration for their captain. When Ambrose was asked what it was like to watch Poulin's standing ovation, a smile came over her face. At the other end of the table in the media room, Poulin looked deeply uncomfortable. "These are my favourite questions. I don't think they're Pou's," Ambrose said. "What happened today and what happens every time that you're in Quebec specifically but anywhere in Canada when Marie-Philip Poulin's name gets called, that is the recognition that this girl deserves. She is the most incredible human being that I have ever been able to be around. She is the best leader."

Poulin mumbled something in protest and sank further into her ball cap as the room of reporters laughed. Ambrose continued. "The best part is that everybody sees it, but it's on a day-to-day basis with Pou, we treat Pou as Pou. We don't need to give her anything. She is who she is, and she's the best human being that we want to be around. She's somebody that makes you a better person. So when people are able to give her that recognition, I don't think it can be done enough. [If] there was a time for me to cry on the blue line, it was probably in that moment because I get to stand beside her, not just as her teammate but as her friend. That means the world to me."

Poulin struggled to find the words to describe what she'd experienced that night, settling on incredible and surreal. "It's been years in the making. We've been striving, we've been wanting to be in that moment, and we're here," she said. For years, people wondered when this league would come. And at first, players wondered when the excitement might die down. But four months in, the excitement only seemed to be growing. It made Poulin emotional. "It's bigger than ourselves."

Four days after the emotion of the Bell Centre game, PWHL Montréal returned to play at Verdun Auditorium for the final time in the season, maybe forever. The rink had all the infrastructure the team needed as a practice facility, and it was a special place to everyone on the team. But selling out the Bell Centre was a sign that more people wanted to see their games. An even surer sign of that was the scalper posted outside Verdun Auditorium before the game. They'd outgrown playing games here.

It was also the team's final home game before the playoffs. Montréal could clinch a playoff spot with a win over New York in regulation that night, among a few other scenarios. New York, meanwhile, was dead last in the league. A regulation loss would eliminate New York from playoff contention. Kori Cheverie expected her team would face a desperate team, and Montréal would need to match that desperation to win. They worked on shot-blocking at practice the day before. The captain set the pace, eagerly blocking every puck a coach threw her way.

Despite the loss against Toronto, the team had seemed to find a groove after the world championship break. The power play was clicking, and several players had come back from worlds with a boost in confidence. Erin Ambrose was one of them. After finding herself on the outside looking in on the first power-play unit with Team Canada, which she had typically anchored, Ambrose had assisted on the game-winning golden goal in the world championship final. Coming back to Montréal, Ambrose recorded five points in two games and was named the league's first star of the week. "I think she's got a little chip on her shoulder, and I like that," Cheverie said at the practice before the New York game. "It's important to take the fuel that you need and implement it into your game, and I think that's what she's doing right now."

The game also marked the return of New York's Jill Saulnier to the arena where she had trained for the last few years alongside Marie-Philip Poulin, Laura Stacey, and Ann-Renée Desbiens. Saulnier once wore on her jersey the Les Canadiennes logo still painted at centre ice. Now, she stood across from those players on the blue line during the national anthems.

New York seized momentum in the first period, thanks to three back-to-back Montréal penalties. But Montréal emerged from the first period with a 1–0 lead, after defender Catherine Daoust's first goal of the season. She fired the puck down the ice, and it bounced off the boards at a weird angle along the way. New York goaltender Corinne Schroeder, thinking the puck was going to travel along the boards, left her crease to play it. Instead, it bounced into her empty net. It was a weird one, but weird goals still count.

The power play hummed along in the second period, with goals on the advantage from Kristin O'Neill and Stacey. In between those goals, Catherine Dubois registered her second marker of the season. A couple of minutes earlier, her heart had sunk when she served her second penalty of the game. She felt like it wasn't going to be her night. But she redeemed herself, and her coach later said she liked how she responded to the adversity. "I was really happy for Dubey—that's what I call her; probably no one else calls her that," Cheverie said after the game. "She knew that she plays on the fourth line. To take two penalties is something that she probably knows she's not supposed to do. To come back and score right away after that second penalty, it truly is the character of that person."

New York clawed back with two goals, one in the dying seconds of the second period from Ella Shelton and another by Quebecer Alexandra Labelle late in the third. But it wasn't enough to dent Montréal's lead. In her final regular-season game at home in Montréal in what would be her final season of professional hockey, veteran Mélodie Daoust buried the empty netter. Montréal officially clinched a playoff spot. The extra work in practice blocking shots that week paid off. Those small details—getting sticks and bodies in front of pucks and in shooting lanes—had helped win this game and would be the kind of habits the team would need to be successful in the playoffs.

When the game ended, the players gathered at centre ice and saluted the crowd with their sticks. Poulin skated to the middle, and her teammates crowded in around her. As most of the players skated away, four stayed behind to dance to "Le bal masqué," as was tradition after a win on home ice. Some of the regulars were on the injured list, so O'Neill was recruited to join the performance. "I was a little lost, to be honest, but I did my best," O'Neill said later. After that, the whole team returned to form a circle around centre ice, just as they'd done back in January when PWHL Montréal played its first game inside this rink. Cheverie and general manager Danièle Sauvageau joined them.

Sauvageau spoke first, thanking the fans as well as the Mark Walter Group and Billie Jean King Enterprises for making the league a reality. She thanked the team's business staff, the people working hard behind the scenes—led by director of business operations Marie-Christine Boucher, known around the rink for making everything run smoothly—for all they'd done this season. Then, as Cheverie took the microphone, the crowd cheered her. "Merci tout le monde," she said. "Très bon." She pointed at a "très bon" sign in the crowd. It had become a catchphrase for the coach throughout the season as she learned French. Her family had even made "très bon" T-shirts, complete with a photo of Cheverie flashing a thumbs up. Then, Poulin took the microphone. She thanked the crowd for the magic and energy they'd brought to their games. "On behalf of the team, we cannot thank you guys enough for coming day in and day out to support us," she said in English.

The loud reception from the fans that night was something Cheverie couldn't have imagined in her early days as Montréal's head coach, when she was under fire for not being able to speak the language. Two days earlier, she'd given her second full interview in French, live on the radio with 98.5 FM host Patrick Lagacé. She often did her French classes on game days to keep her mind, and her French talking points, fresh.

"I don't think I realized at the beginning first of all how hard it is to be a head coach in a major city, and then to be the head coach in Montréal where you don't speak the language," Cheverie said after the win over New York. "And then obviously I think back now, and our power play sucked at the beginning. All of these things we've gone through as a team. It feels like we've lived an entire lifetime in one year. I'm really proud of our group and proud of the perseverance."

Her team would enjoy the win, but there was lots of work left to do. Montréal had two regular-season games left before the playoffs began. Asked if she planned to rest any of her star players, Cheverie laughed. It was important to keep players sharp heading into the playoffs. Too much rest could be a bad thing. "We'll see how the minutes go. But I don't think I'm going to tell Pou she's not playing." For the players, the prospect of playing playoff games in front of a fired-up Montréal crowd was exciting. Dubois quipped that they were doing something the men couldn't, referring to the Montréal Canadiens missing the playoffs. She and the rest of the media room laughed, but she seemed to regret the joke as soon as it came out of her mouth. She showed up to her team's next game wearing a Habs jersey.

16
CHASING THE WALTER CUP

May 4, 2024
Lowell, Massachusetts

Montréal's last game of the regular season was on the road at the Tsongas Center in Lowell, Massachusetts, the rink more than half an hour outside of Boston that serves as that PWHL team's home. Even though they were hours away from Montréal, the players stepped off the bus that afternoon to a line of Montréal fans cheering and waving signs. Some, like Josée-Anne Nantel-Legault and Shanee Lafortune, drove nearly five hours to get to this game. The friends, who'd met at a PWHL Montréal game, had planned the trip earlier in the week, after running into each other at an away game in Ottawa. They left Montréal at seven that morning and planned to drive back through the night.

Both had started following PWHL Montréal at the beginning of the season and watched the city embrace the team. They heard more and more people talking about the league, and they watched even the games at the larger Place Bell begin to sell out. The impact of that had hit Lafortune at the last game she'd attended, when she talked to a mother about how her daughter will grow up not knowing anything different than this level of attention and exposure for female hockey players. It will be the norm for her. "It's long due," Lafortune said.

Montréal had already clinched a playoff spot, but this game would determine the fate of PWHL Boston. The team needed to beat Montréal in regulation and have Minnesota lose its game against New York that day in regulation in order to make the playoffs. Boston had been a different team since the world championship break, and they weren't going to go easily. The crowd watching them that day was the biggest one PWHL Boston had drawn to the Tsongas Center all season long. The game was sold out even though the Bruins were playing a playoff game seven against the Toronto Maple Leafs in downtown Boston a few hours later. By the time the puck dropped on the PWHL game, fans had snapped up all the adult-sized PWHL jerseys on sale. And Boston got the first bit of help it would need to make the playoffs, although the players wouldn't learn about it until after their game: two minutes before Boston's game with Montréal started, New York beat Minnesota 5–2. Boston's fate was in their hands now. Montréal wasn't going to make it easy, though. Each one of the team's stars was playing that afternoon.

Boston's determination shone through at the beginning of the game as the team built a 3–0 lead going into the third period. Before the third began, two women proposed to each other at centre ice after taking part in a shooting competition, to the delight of the crowd.

Mikyla Grant-Mentis, the player Montréal had picked up off waivers in March, made things interesting in the third. A member of the second power-play unit, she scored on the advantage twice in less than eight minutes. With three and a half minutes left and her team trailing 3–2, Kori Cheverie pulled goaltender Ann-Renée Desbiens. Her team's season wasn't on the line, but the coach still hates losing.

After a pass from Erin Ambrose, timed for when Marie-Philip Poulin could find some space, the captain—who had been throwing her body around all afternoon long—fired a shot on Boston goalie

Aerin Frankel and then put her own rebound into the net, tying the game. Montréal looked to have put a dagger in Boston's season. Montréal fans were elated. Boston fans, knowing how much the team needed a regulation win, looked stressed.

"There's no one like Pou. They call her Captain Clutch for a reason," Cheverie said later. "She honestly does step up in those moments where you need her to. That's why she's arguably the best player in the world, because she has the game on her stick. She's able to make you pay."

With less than a minute and a half to play, Boston defender Kaleigh Fratkin saved the team's playoff hopes with an innocent-looking shot from the top of the right circle that beat Desbiens. Cheverie pulled Desbiens again, and in the scrambly final seconds of the game, it looked like Montréal could pull off more extra-attacker magic. But it wasn't meant to be. Boston won 4–3 and clinched a playoff spot. Poulin finished the game with eight shots.

As the Montréal players spoke to reporters after the game, you could hear the Boston players celebrating, likely enjoying the cart of champagne that had been wheeled into the locker room minutes earlier. "We knew that nothing today was going to change our fate and where we were," Ambrose said of the team's mentality before the game. "It's hard to match somebody who's playing for their season." That showed in the first two periods, she said, as the team fell into a 3–0 hole. But something switched in the team going into the third. The leaders in the room spoke up. The team needed to play the third in the way they wanted to go into the playoffs, they said: more desperate, more physical.

Though Poulin scored the tying goal, Grant-Mentis, the player Ottawa had let go just a couple of months earlier, fuelled the comeback. The player who teammates call Buckey brought spirit to the locker room, Ambrose said. "The girl had a bit of a tough road. She could have easily come in and been quiet and in the corner, but she's been a lot of light in our dressing room, a lot of fun for us to be around." Ambrose also recognized Grant-Mentis's natural talent. "Season opener for us in Ottawa, [we] saw Buckey's skill," she said. "It's not fun to play against."

The game wrapped up a couple of hours before the Bruins–Leafs game began in the city. As they left the room filled with Boston reporters, Ambrose whispered, "Go Leafs go."

"Go Leafs go!" Grant-Mentis said with more enthusiasm.

"I didn't say it that loud for everybody to hear," Ambrose said.

"Say it louder," Grant-Mentis responded.

"In front of the media! You're sewering me, Buckey."

After the players got dressed, Poulin spent time meeting with kids inside the rink. Outside, a crowd of fans waited at the Montréal bus to greet the players as they left. Many stopped to pose for pictures and sign autographs. Grant-Mentis found her family in the crowd outside, including her mother, who was wearing a Leafs jersey in enemy territory. The player watched the scene from afar with her post-game meal and a book her mother brought her in hand, encouraging a fan who wondered whether she should yell a compliment at Montréal's Leah Lum. It was another sign of how far this league and team had come, how its popularity had surged. They were celebrities even as the away team.

A few days later, Toronto, which finished first atop the PWHL standings and earned the right to pick its first-round playoff opponent between the third- and fourth-seeded teams, announced it would play Minnesota. Montréal finished the regular season second in the standings, six points behind first-place Toronto. That meant the team got home-ice advantage and would start the playoffs at Place Bell, the bigger arena that would host all of Montréal's at-home playoff games. It also meant Montréal and Boston would see a lot more of each other over the next few days, as they'd be playoff opponents. Each round of the playoffs would be a best-of-five series. If the regular-season finale was any indication, a series between Boston and Montréal was going to be physical and fast.

The last time Marie-Philip Poulin had played in a professional league playoff series was with Les Canadiennes in 2019. Then, Boston captain Hilary Knight was her teammate. She and Knight had taken a moment to hug on the ice after their teams' regular-season finale. "It's always such an honour to play against Hilary Knight, because there's such a respect there for what she's done for women's hockey, for what she's done for hockey," Poulin told reporters before their playoff series began. "The way we play on the ice, we're not friends out there. But when it's time to shake hands, there's a lot of respect there."

Now, two of the biggest stars in women's hockey—one Canadian, one American—were set to face off in the playoffs. Poulin expected it to be a battle, just as physical as the last game of the regular season. Montréal would need to face Boston goaltender Aerin Frankel, the Team USA starter whose play had kept Boston afloat throughout the season when the team struggled to score. It would be a grind. Best-of-five was longer than anyone was used to playing in a playoff series. But it was also exciting, especially for the players who hadn't competed in a league for several years. This was what they'd worked for all season long. "We've been waiting for that moment since the season opener back in January," Poulin said. "This league has been unbelievable to be part of. Every day, it's been competitive."

A month earlier, the league had unveiled the trophy the teams were

Marie-Philip Poulin and Ann-Renée Desbiens chat before a game in Ottawa at the end of the regular season, just before Montréal starts the Walter Cup playoffs. (Ellen Bond Photo)

competing to win. The Walter Cup was a nod to the Walter family that had made the league a reality. Billie Jean King had suggested the name. "The Walter Cup marks a monumental milestone in women's hockey and for all women's sports," King said in a press release when the trophy was unveiled. "It recognizes the historic commitment by Mark and Kimbra Walter to make this dream come true for the PWHL players of today and tomorrow."

The sterling silver cup, designed in collaboration with the luxury jeweller Tiffany & Co., weighs about thirty-five pounds and stands twenty-four inches tall. The base features an image of a puck smashing a glass ceiling and a place for the winning team's name. The trophy then juts into a V-shape, with the design of a hockey stick on either side, each etched with a pattern of skate marks on the back. The V of sticks supports a bowl at the top of the trophy, which is engraved with six PWHL logos along with rays of light, signifying the six founding teams and the dawn of a new era of women's hockey. The Walter Cup gave PWHL players their own trophy to work toward winning—just as players in the CWHL had fought for the Clarkson Cup, and teams in the PHF had competed to win the Isobel Cup.

For Montréal, the next step in that quest began on May 9, a Thursday night, inside Place Bell, where more than nine thousand people showed up to cheer on their team in game one against Boston. Montréal threw everything at Boston goaltender Frankel that night, fifty-four shots in total, in what was a chippy, somewhat oddly officiated game. Laura Stacey had a number of good chances, including one on a power play. Frankel made a massive stretch save. On another chance, Stacey had a good look at the net before Frankel's stick flew out of her hands at Stacey. No official called a penalty on Frankel. "She didn't throw her stick," Kori Cheverie said after the game with a straight face. "That's what I was told."

Despite the opportunities, only Kristin O'Neill beat Frankel when she tipped Stacey's shot on a power play in the second. But less than two minutes into the third, Boston's Lexie Adzija tied it. The game was just as physical as many had predicted, and players were going to have to summon a bit more energy for overtime—especially the team's stars, on whom Cheverie relied heavily in that game. Poulin, O'Neill, Stacey, and Erin Ambrose finished the game with more than half an hour of ice time each. No one on the fourth line played a single shift.

Montréal had a golden opportunity when Boston defender Megan Keller went off for slashing in overtime, but they couldn't put a puck past Frankel. More than fourteen minutes into the extra period, Boston's Susanna Tapani ended it on a play that started with a turnover behind Montréal's net and finished with a scramble in front of Desbiens. Montréal had been close all game, but it wasn't enough.

After the game, both Cheverie and Poulin mentioned the consistency of the officiating, questioning why something might be called a penalty in one game and not in another—a common concern as the league seemed to still be figuring out officiating. But the coach said the team couldn't dwell on the disappointment of losing in overtime. "We had our opportunities to score," Cheverie told reporters. "Obviously we need to put a couple of those in. It's disappointing.... But if I look at the game as a whole, I'm happy with what our group did, what they were able to achieve in this game, and I think that gives us momentum moving forward."

Little did they know that lots more extra hockey awaited them in game two.

Two days later, on a Saturday night, Boston and Montréal were back at Place Bell for a rematch in front of a sold-out crowd of more than ten thousand. A five-game series sounds long, compared to previous leagues where playoff rounds were decided in three games or sometimes just one. For the players, it probably felt long, too. But in reality, there wasn't much room for error. Lose two in a row and you've dug a hole.

Seven minutes in, Amanda Pelkey opened the scoring for Boston when her shot from behind the net deflected past goalie Ann-Renée Desbiens. For the second game in a row, Kristin O'Neill on the power play tied the game after Aerin Frankel lost control of the puck in her crease and O'Neill got her stick on it. And for the second game in a row, this thing was headed to overtime. A few minutes into the extra frame, Boston's Lexie Adzija received a game misconduct for a hit on Laura Stacey. She was done for the game, and Montréal had a five-minute advantage. They still couldn't solve Frankel. The game continued on with Boston getting a power play to begin the second overtime, but their players couldn't beat Desbiens.

It took until more than halfway through the third overtime for Boston fourth-liner Taylor Wenczkowski, left alone for a few seconds in front of Desbiens, to finally end it. Just like that, Montréal was down 2–0 in the series and players on both sides had some serious recovery to do before travelling to Boston for game three.

Marie-Philip Poulin, Stacey, and O'Neill all played more than fifty minutes while Erin Ambrose logged an astounding sixty-one minutes. By the end, coach Kori Cheverie said she struggled to remember who'd just come off the ice and what situation they were in. The game had gone so long that by the time the players left the rink, Montréal's Leah Lum and Boston's Abby Cook were a year older than when they started the game. Montréal had again managed more than fifty shots, but Frankel and Desbiens had put on a clinic. Asked whether she felt more players had to contribute offensively, Cheverie reminded everyone that Boston had scored only one more goal than Montréal in both games. "We're already having good conversations with the coaches in the dressing room," she told reporters. "Our plan is already in place of what we need to tackle for game three.... It's not like it was 4–0 and 3–0 games. It could have went either way. And so when that happens, as much as you hate to lose, you have to move forward and be okay. It's one mistake here, one mistake here, one decision there that makes a difference. So, for us, I'm not worried."

Stacey stayed positive, too, but she looked defeated in the post-game press conference. Playing fifty-two minutes will do that to you. "We recently had somebody come in and talk to us, and they told us when your body's giving out or when you don't feel like you have anything left physically, that's when you've got to pull through. You never know what you have left inside you," Stacey said, her voice breaking. "And I think that's what we just kept saying to ourselves in the locker room, on the benches. It hurts. It doesn't feel nice. But let's just keep pushing and doing whatever we can mentally to get through this." Everyone knew that one bounce, one mental lapse, is all it takes for a game and a playoff series to slip away.

Despite the pressure of being down 2–0 in a playoff series, Poulin made time to have a special moment with a young fan before game three. She ran over to meet a young girl named Constance who had travelled from Quebec City to Lowell to cheer on her favourite team. Poulin gave Constance a big hug in a moment the team captured. Then she kneeled down to chat with her, thanking her for coming to their game and for pictures the girl drew for her. No matter how many demands Poulin has on her time—demands that will only continue to grow as a face of a growing league—she always takes an extra moment to meet young girls, always appreciating the spark in their eyes when they talk to her. A couple of months earlier in Verdun, the team recorded her as she popped out of the locker room to meet a fan who held a sign saying she wanted to be Poulin when she grew up. "That's awesome. And guess what? You're way better than that," Poulin told the girl. "Be yourself."

Poulin has always thrived in big games, and this game was the biggest one she would play all season. Lose and the team would be done for the season. Win and they still had a shot at making the Walter Cup final. Less than sixteen minutes into the game, Poulin opened the scoring on a pass from Mikyla Grant-Mentis. She was new to Poulin's line that night. Kori Cheverie thought her vision and ability to find open ice could spark something. If there was a time to try something new, it was now, with the season on the line.

Montréal took a 2–0 lead into the third period off a deflected shot from Maureen Murphy on the power play. It was the rookie's first career playoff goal. It felt like momentum was on Montréal's side, having beat Aerin Frankel twice. But a few minutes into the third period, Boston cut the lead in half on a goal from Sophie Shirley. The dagger came with less than four minutes left, when Boston's Amanda Pelkey—the same player who'd spoiled Montréal's home opener back in January—tied it on a shorthanded breakaway. After celebrating the jailbreak goal, the Boston players skated over to call for teammate Alina Müller to be freed from the penalty box. Müller hugged Pelkey when she was let out.

For the third game in the series, Boston and Montréal needed overtime. Fortunately for everyone, this one didn't last three periods. It took only one minute and two seconds for Boston's Susanna Tapani, the overtime hero from game one, to score. The initial shot came from Müller. Desbiens made the save but couldn't get back into position in time to save the rebound, which went directly to Tapani's stick. The Boston players flooded the ice to celebrate in front of their home crowd.

It didn't matter that Boston had made it into the playoffs by virtue of a buzzer-beater goal on the last game of the season. It didn't matter that Montréal threw more shots at Frankel in all three games. Any team could win on any day in the PWHL, because the teams were so even, and this was proof. Frankel looked unbeatable at times, which earned her the nickname "the green monster," a reference to the colour of Boston's jerseys. Three of Montréal's four goals in the series came from its top power-play unit, while the fourth line played sparingly throughout the series. Meanwhile, Boston got key goals from its depth players, including Pelkey and game-two goal-scorer Taylor Wenczkowski. Finding depth beyond the team's stars was an area of weakness Montréal would work to address in the off-season.

In the media room after the game, Desbiens, Cheverie, and forward Sarah Lefort looked dejected. Desbiens wiped tears from her eyes as her coach tried her hardest to keep it together. Cheverie told reporters the group was still trying to process everything. She wanted her players to know how well they played over the three games and that it was okay to feel the emotion. It was important to feel it. A reporter asked Cheverie what had happened to her team in the third period, when Montréal's 2–0 lead evaporated. "I don't think that there was much difference," she said. "I mean, you obviously had a team on the other side who was pushing back. I don't know if they matched our push in the first two [periods], and then in the third, they decided they wanted to win in sixty, I guess, and they had that pushback. I think out of the...how many periods did we play? Twelve? I would say we probably outplayed them for ten. It wasn't quite enough."

Even though they were on the road, Desbiens thanked the fans back home in Montréal, who had shown up for them all season long, the fans she described as the best in the league. "We do have the loudest building in the league," Cheverie said. "Sorry, Boston people, but we do." Being a part of the team had been special, the coach said, whether it was the players on the ice or the healthy scratches in the stands. "We had a really special group, so..." the coach said, choking up too much to finish her sentence. Later that night, just before midnight, Amy Scheer's phone buzzed inside her Massachusetts hotel room. It was a message from Poulin. Amid her disappointment, the captain thanked the league's senior vice-president of business operations for all the work she'd done that season.

The players would head back to Montréal and, a few days later, clean out their lockers. Some had played their last game in a Montréal jersey. Others had played their last game in the PWHL. Lefort and Mélodie Daoust were among the players who stepped away from playing pro hockey. Leah Lum and Jillian Dempsey, who'd played sparingly through the playoffs, signed elsewhere in the off-season: Lum with a team in China, and Dempsey as a reserve back at home in Boston. Sarah Bujold, who'd scored in the Bell Centre game, went into the next season in Montréal without a contract. When she didn't make the team out of training camp, she signed in Sweden. But many would be back the next year to take another shot at winning the Walter Cup, including the core of the team, led by their captain. Catherine Dubois signed a one-year deal to come back, ensuring she wouldn't have to start the next season living with the uncertainty of being on the reserve list. Several players stuck around Montréal for the summer, training at Centre 21.02.

"I'm proud of what we've accomplished, even if the road ended sooner than we'd hoped," Poulin wrote on social media a few days after the loss. "I have learned over the years that defeat is not synonymous with failure. Setbacks allow us to grow, to understand what we need to work on to improve. Failure is part of success, in sport as in life. I want all the young girls watching us to understand that on the road to success, there will be obstacles, but they can be overcome with hard work and determination." The captain thanked her teammates, coaches, and support staff as well as the fans for supporting them throughout the season. "I am grateful to everyone who showed support during our inaugural PWHL season," she wrote. "You thrilled us with your energy and enthusiasm. I've said it before, and I'll say it again: we have the best fans. Thank you Montréal, see you next season."

17
CROWNING A CHAMPION
May 2024

After four periods of scoreless hockey, it looked like Minnesota had just won the Walter Cup. Rookie defender Sophie Jaques scored, and the Minnesota bench erupted, sending sticks and gloves flying all over the ice at the Xcel Energy Center.

Advisory board members Stan Kasten, Billie Jean King, and Ilana Kloss sat with Jayna Hefford inside the rink, watching the game. Everyone started scurrying around to get ready for the trophy presentation. But Kasten remembers Hefford turning to him and telling him she didn't think the goal would count. She was right. After a lengthy review, the league's central situation room overturned the goal due to goaltender interference. Before Jaques's shot, her teammate, Taylor Heise, had slid into Boston's Aerin Frankel. The officials determined that Heise had gone into the goalie "on her own volition," not because of another player, which meant Frankel couldn't play and defend the shot. After the emotion of celebrating a championship, the Minnesota players had to collect their equipment off the ice and go back to playing.

Less than a minute of play later, Boston's Alina Müller scored to force a game five back in Boston. After her goal, Müller raced off the ice and down the tunnel, as if she had forgotten to do something important. Behind the scenes, league staff had to hustle to get everything they'd prepared for a trophy presentation that night, including the Walter Cup itself, into a van, which was then driven to Boston.

About five minutes after game four ended, Kasten got a text from Mark Walter. "I'll see you Wednesday in Boston," he wrote. The schedule hadn't worked out for the Walters to see a PWHL game in person yet, but they knew if the series stretched to a deciding fifth and final game, they would be able to make it. Their first PWHL game would be the championship, and it would also be the first time they saw the Walter Cup in person.

That night, Minnesota won the championship—for real this time—defeating Boston 3–0. Heise, the league's first draft pick in 2023, was named the Ilana Kloss Playoff MVP. Kloss, with Kasten and advisory board member Royce Cohen flanking her, handed Heise the trophy. When it was time to award the Walter Cup, two Hockey Hall of Fame staff donned white gloves to carefully remove it from a big teal Tiffany box in the arena hallway. Together, they carefully carried it down the carpet and onto the ice, where they placed it on a table covered with a black sheet as the Minnesota players looked on with excitement, some wiping away tears. Mark and Kimbra Walter followed, their first public appearance in the league they'd created. King and Hefford followed them, arm in arm as they had been at the league's first game back on January 1.

"On behalf of the league, I'd like to thank all the fans who've made this year unbelievable, made our finals an incredible five-game set," Mark Walter told the crowd. "And we really appreciate the support and love you've given all the teams and all the players. I'd like to congratulate Boston on an incredible season and an incredibly well-fought final playoff. Now we'd like to congratulate Minnesota for winning the inaugural season Walter Cup."

Hefford also thanked the fans who attended or watched the league's games that season and congratulated both teams before passing the microphone to King. "The Walter family are leaders in philanthropy and business, but they were willing to invest in the PWHL, the dream," King said. "So I'm honoured to present this trophy alongside Mark and Kimbra Walter." With that, she introduced Minnesota captain Kendall Coyne Schofield. Mark Walter passed Coyne Schofield the cup and she became the first player to lift it. She raised it over her head less than a year after giving birth to her son, Drew, who would celebrate on the ice that night with his mom. On the other side of Coyne Schofield was King, one of Coyne Schofield's first calls at the beginning of this idea to start something new, and a champion of the plan from the beginning.

The PWHL staff had done many walkthroughs of the trophy presentation, rehearsing the order and how things would go. But nothing could really prepare them for the moment. Hefford tried to absorb everything, from the reaction of the players to, later, their families on the ice with them. Hefford's own family was able to be there that night to celebrate with her.

"For Kendall to be able to win the first one, you can't really write a story like that," Hefford said in an interview months later. "She is more responsible than any player for making this happen. I have so much respect for her in what she's done and how she's gone about it."

In June, the league returned to Minnesota for a couple of days to hold its second draft and first awards ceremony. The league was in the midst of its first real controversy. Days before the draft, Minnesota GM Natalie Darwitz and the organization had parted ways. The questions about her departure and what prompted it put a damper on the team's championship celebration. When head coach Ken Klee ran the team's draft in Darwitz's absence, some Minnesota fans in attendance booed him. Later that night, the coach faced more questions after drafting Britta Curl, a Team USA player whose social media activity had drawn attention. Curl had liked a post that called Target a "perverted company" and called for it to be boycotted for selling 2SLGBTQIA+-themed products. She'd liked another post about a not-guilty verdict for Kyle Rittenhouse, who was charged with shooting three men, two fatally, during a Black Lives Matter protest. Curl later apologized. "I specifically recognize that my social media activity has resulted in hurt being felt across communities including LGBTQ+ and BIPOC individuals, and I just want to apologize and take ownership of that," Curl said in a video posted to her social media. Montréal, meanwhile, used its first-round pick that night to draft defender Cayla Barnes. Already an Olympic gold medallist from 2018 with Team USA, Barnes gave Montréal another bona fide top-four defender who could ease some of the load on Erin Ambrose.

The next day, the league held its award banquet. Marie-Philip Poulin, who had finished the season tied for second in the league with twenty-three points in twenty-one games, was nominated for both the Billie Jean King MVP Award and Forward of the Year. She lost both to Toronto's Natalie Spooner, who'd had a dominant season, just a little over a year after giving birth to her son, Rory. Kori Cheverie was nominated for Coach of the Year after leading Montréal to second place in the league, despite a long list of players lost to injury. She had also led her team to a turnaround on the power play, which significantly improved after the world championship break. Her fellow Nova Scotian Troy Ryan took home the award. He had taken Toronto from worst in the league to best, winning eleven games in a row in the middle of the regular season.

The league hadn't listed who was up for its Hockey for All Award, a Scotiabank-sponsored prize for the league's humanitarian of the year. The award went to Montréal rookie Maureen Murphy in recognition of her work with several different organizations, including the geriatric hospitals she'd visited throughout the season. While adjusting to pro hockey and doing law classes on the side, Murphy and her dog, Bean, had managed to fit in more than two hundred hours of volunteer work. "We had some ups and downs this year," Murphy told reporters after the ceremony. "I think it's a great reminder for all athletes that you're a person first.... I'd love to play hockey forever, but that's not realistic. So I think [I'm] kind of doing the best of both worlds."

"I am so happy that she got the recognition," her teammate Ambrose said, adding that Murphy had become one of her closest friends on the team this season. "I know that I should be joining her at some of her volunteer times, because as much as Maureen will say it was all Bean, her dog, that made the difference, Maureen really does impact people and make people's lives brighter on a day-to-day basis." Ambrose also brought home an award that day. She won Defender of the Year over New York's Ella Shelton and Boston's Megan Keller. Montréal had relied on her in all situations throughout the season. This recognition came five years after she won the same award in the last season of the CWHL, wearing a different Montréal sweater. So much had changed for Ambrose in that time, but Montréal would always tie those years together, from when this city helped her find her way back onto the ice to being thirty years old and an Olympic champion. "For me, I think some things had to happen in my life, some disappointments in my career," Ambrose said that day, as she reflected on the five years that had passed. "And I'd like to say that it's kind of turned things in the right direction for me. Obviously making an Olympic team, winning some world championships, getting drafted to

Montréal, having this great season. It's hard to kind of put into words, because part of me doesn't really realize what I've done and what I've accomplished in the last five years. But if you ask me when I'm forty, I will probably say that this is one of the most impactful five years of my life." In that first professional season, Ambrose learned she could be a good pro. She also learned what she needed to do outside the rink to handle her off days and be the best version of herself.

"I think at the beginning of the year, I was struggling to find my footing a little bit and my consistency," Ambrose said. "I pride myself immensely on being a consistent player, and it was just the ins and outs of day-to-day practices that I needed to get a little bit more consistent in to take my game to the next level. I think it's just a matter of continuing to understand that and continuing to see what I need as an individual athlete, because it's not the same as what other people on the team need." As much as the individual honour meant to her, the trophy she really wanted to lift that season was the Walter Cup. Not having won made everything bittersweet.

For months after Ambrose and Team Canada lost the 2023 world championship to the Americans, Ambrose had hung her silver medal on a door to give her a visual reminder of finishing second and the drive to be golden the next year. Ambrose scored a goal in the gold-medal game against the United States in 2024 and then assisted on Danielle Serdachny's gold-winning overtime goal. Just as silver had stung in 2023, the disappointment of losing to Boston wasn't going to go away anytime soon. You don't have to look far inside Centre 21.02 to see the standard set in Montréal. It's on display in the championship team photos and the banners that sit in the trophy case not far from the rink where the Montréal players practise. "It's going to be pretty easy to get motivated this summer," Ambrose said. "There's a lot that

I want to accomplish as an individual athlete to make sure that I can best impact Montréal to bring back a Walter Cup."

That journey to the next Walter Cup playoffs began with off-season training in Verdun with many of her teammates. That summer, there'd be no lingering questions about how the league would look or where Ambrose would play the next season. Montréal would be her home.

EPILOGUE
VICTOIRE DE MONTRÉAL

September 2024

Marie-Philip Poulin took time away from a Hockey Canada camp to hop on a Zoom call. When she joined, she was wearing a brand-new red T-shirt with *Montréal Victoire* written on it.

After a season as PWHL Montréal, the team finally had a name and a logo, something new to weave into the team's identity. The work to design six logos and choose team names occurred throughout the first season. The year before, six prospective names had leaked through trademark filings, prompting fans and commentators to pan them on social media. The league ended up rejecting all six of those names. This time around, the league successfully kept all six team names and logos under wraps and unveiled them on the same day in September 2024. In addition to the Victoire, the Ottawa Charge, Toronto Sceptres, New York Sirens, Minnesota Frost, and Boston Fleet were announced.

The criteria for a good name were that it inspired pride of place, captured the soul of the city, and connected with fans, the league's vice-president of brand and marketing, Kanan Bhatt-Shah, told reporters on the day the names and logos were unveiled. When considering each potential identity for a team, they thought about how it could come to life in the arena and whether it would resonate with fans after a year of getting to know each team's fanbase. It also had to be something new so the league could own it, trademark it, and build its own history. That ruled out names used in the CWHL or the PHF.

A purposely small group within the PWHL workshopped hundreds of names. Victoire made everyone around the table smile as soon as it came up. The name translates to victory in English, but the league decided that sticking with a French name would be the best way to represent Montréal and Quebec. "When we saw that name, we all loved it," Amy Scheer, the league's senior vice-president of business operations, said on the day the league announced the team names. "We felt it really talked to the essence of Montréal as a city, to the people of the city, and their expectations for championships, given their rich history in sports. I think it was one of those names that when it hit you, you felt immediately good about it." Victoire represents Montréal's "joyously competitive spirit" and mindset of wanting to achieve the best. Montréal's new logo features a hidden *M* and the national symbol, the fleur-de-lis, in the middle. The logo appears to have wings, a nod to the Goddess of Victory and a representation of "strength and agility." The league kept each team's colours from the first season and designed logos to match, meaning Montréal would continue to wear maroon. The team debuted new jerseys for season two with those new logos.

Just as the league intended with the name, Poulin said Victoire would be the Montréal players' mindset. But a new name and logo on their jerseys wouldn't change what the leaders on this team had built inside the locker room the season before. "Every day, you want to perform, you want to bring out your best, and it's just going to be what our team is going to rally around, what the city is going to rally around, what our fans are going to be all about," Poulin said. It also opened up the possibility for Montréal to get its own mascot. Asked to come up with an idea, Poulin said she felt like it should have wings, given the team's logo. "We've been waiting for that moment," she said. "Now we have logos, names, and obviously mascots are going to come. It's going to be all new to us, and it's going to be exciting."

Months after she sat between her two devastated players after the first-round playoff loss to Boston, Kori Cheverie still replayed the images of heartbreak on her players' faces, the pain they felt that night. But she was at peace with the way her team's season ended. That doesn't mean she liked it. She hates to lose. But there's more to coaching than counting wins and losses. There are real people involved, and changing the outcome for the people in that room drove her during her first real off-season in Montréal. "You can beat yourself up as a coach in those moments as well, but you've also got to turn the page and learn from what you'd do differently, learn from what you'd keep the same," she said in an interview months after the loss, after everything had had time to sink in. "A big part of it as well was, how do you deal with losing?"

Cheverie had been an assistant coach at the university level and in the pressure-filled environments of an Olympics and world championship before taking the Montréal job. But the PWHL was the first time she was the head coach of a pro team. She'd found herself in what might be the most passionate women's hockey market. She'd learned how to navigate that while learning French. That first season taught her how she wants to operate as a coach and how she wants to lead her coaching staff.

"Before you're a head coach, you don't fully know, exactly," Cheverie said. "You know bits and pieces, because you know how you show up every day as an assistant coach. But until you're a head coach, you don't see the bigger picture, the thirty-thousand-foot view of how everything has to operate. I think I've learned a lot just in how to manage people and how to really make an organization work with you only being a part of it." She'd learned how to prepare differently over the grind of a season. As her preparation changed, so did her expectations and standards. The numbers said the team was supposed to win the three playoff games they lost. Cheverie said the team's expected goals—a measurement of how likely a shot will result in a goal—were well above the team's actual goals all season.

That told her the team was generating quality chances, that statistically, her team was likely to win games by playing that way—but for many Montréal fans, the only numbers that matter are the number of actual goals, and the score at the end of the game. "The fact that we put together our three best games at the end of the year in playoffs when it mattered, and the difference between every single game came down to one tiny mistake or one bobbled puck? That's what keeps me going with this upcoming year. That's what motivates me."

It didn't take away the pain of losing, but it offered something to focus on to move forward: the prospect of winning a championship in a place that loves women's hockey. As a coach, that's the dream.

Only a few months old, the PWHL still had growing pains to address going into season two, but it would have a bit more runway to figure them out than in season one.

The league lost money in its first year—a lot, according to advisory board member Stan Kasten, who didn't specify an exact number. Starting a new league is expensive. The plan is to build a sustainable business model, which will take time, even if the first season surpassed expectations. But there's no more denying people are interested in watching women's hockey. The league has the numbers to back that up. "Long-term, we've made it clear this works as a business. It works as entertainment," Kasten said in the summer of 2024, as he reflected on the PWHL's whirlwind first year of existence.

The league saw more interest than expected for merchandise in season one, and it wasn't prepared for the demand. It surged again in September 2024 when the teams got names and logos, and then the league had an even better sales day when new Bauer jerseys were unveiled in November 2024. For the first time, fans could buy pro women's hockey merchandise at their local sporting goods store. And this time, the league wanted to make sure there weren't supply issues.

Even though records were broken in season one, and the league saw lots of demand in Canada, there was a lot more room for growth south of the border. New York and Boston drew smaller crowds than the other four markets. The league also lacked a national US television rights deal going into season two. On the ice, the league was still figuring out how to navigate a women's pro hockey league with so much physicality. Making sure everyone knew how to properly take and give a hit, including players who hadn't grown up playing with hitting, and to do that as the game kept getting faster, would take time. So would finding consistency in officiating, a common concern among players in season one.

But there were lots of reasons for optimism. On the ice, all the games were close, adding some extra excitement. Off the ice, the first season was such a success that the league started accepting proposals to expand by as many as two teams as early as the third season. Plenty of cities in both Canada and the United States wanted to host the

PWHL, and nine were chosen to host neutral-site games throughout the second season. Other leagues have experimented with the idea, including the NHL, which has played some regular-season games in Europe. But it was obvious the PWHL games were more than a one-off in a given city. For some, it would be a test of sorts to see if that city could someday be home to a PWHL team.

For many of the women who spent years toiling in leagues that came before the PWHL, that people are interested in women's hockey isn't a surprise. They always knew how great the product on the ice was. The problem was a lack of investment and a lack of public awareness, compounded by little media coverage of the actual hockey being played. While the players valued being role models, they'd too often face more questions about how it felt to be an inspiration to young girls than about the game they'd played. The coverage of women's hockey grew significantly when the PWHL started, but there were still few people able to cover the league for a living. Many, like Montréal's Jared Book, still did it on top of their day jobs, spending their own money and showing up because they love it.

A year into the league's existence, women were making money to play hockey. But for some, it wasn't a livable wage in a major city, and it was a far cry from what men make in the NHL. There is still a long way to go before women's accomplishments on the ice are celebrated the way men's accomplishments are and their labour is valued equally. But the narrative is starting to shift.

Perhaps no one knew that better than Jayna Hefford, who lived it in every way: from being one of the best to play the game in leagues that didn't pay, to shutting down a league she loved, to working to make a business a case for professional women's hockey, to building a brand-new league from the ground up, to then watching it, up close, as it succeeded in year one.

"I don't think we have made it yet," Hefford said a few months before the league would begin its second season. "But I think we couldn't have asked for a better first season. Now our challenge is to do it again, bigger and better."

ACKNOWLEDGEMENTS

I wouldn't have written this book if it weren't for my late grandfather, John "Papa Jack" Donkin. We spent so many hours watching hockey games together, and when he became too sick to watch in person, we listened on the radio or watched on TV. I know he would have loved to read this book. Thank you for helping me fall in love with this amazing game.

I'm grateful to everyone at Goose Lane Editions, including Simon Thibault, Susanne Alexander, and Alan Sheppard, for believing in this project. There aren't many books about women's hockey. I hope there will be many more someday. Thank you to my editors, Jill Ainsley and Jess Shulman, for spending so many hours making this book exponentially better. I couldn't be more grateful for your careful eye. I am also appreciative to BB Burnett and Jeff Arbeau, who helped get this book in more hands.

To Lauren Bird, who let me write so much of this book at her kitchen table when I needed a change of scenery, I will always be grateful to you.

Thank you to the many people who offered advice to me as a first-time author, who offered their homes to me on reporting trips or just went above and beyond to offer support. There are too many to name, but they include Jacques Poitras, Angela Gilbert, the White House girls, Joey O'Kane, Mackenzie Shaw, Josh O'Kane, Colleen

Kitts-Goguen, Darcy Shea, Marty Klinkenberg, Sean Fitz-Gerald, Jan Wong, Bobbi-Jean MacKinnon, Erin Valois, Ailish Forfar, Jared Book, Alex Azzi, Kamila Hinkson, Christine Roger, Grace Annear, and Meaghan Mayo. Special thanks to Richard Scott for always being a great resource, and for meticulously saving and generously sharing so many photos of this game over the years.

I'm grateful to the teams at CBC New Brunswick and CBC Sports for allowing me to pursue this project, and for allowing the use of some material I gathered at the 2023 PWHL Draft. Special thank you to Ryan Johnston, Victoria Goodfellow Nicholls, Patrick Grier, Tony Care, Chris Sullivan, Chris Wilson, Vanessa Campion, and Darrow MacIntyre.

Thank you to the folks with the PWHPA, the PWHL, and the Montréal Victoire for making this project possible. Special thanks to Charles Rooke, Paul Krotz, Mandy Gutmann, Marie-Christine Boucher, Ashley McLellan, Jana Arbour, Liz Knox, Danièle Sauvageau, and Kori Cheverie. I appreciate all the players who took the time to share their stories. There are many more than those who are named in these pages. Every conversation was important and helped me understand the reality of their world.

Thank you to the great group of PWHL reporters in Montréal who welcomed me into your circle. You're the best.

Finally, a big thank you to everyone who has covered and documented women's hockey history over the years, often for little to no compensation. If not for Richard Scott, Jared Book, Hailey Salvian, The Ice Garden, *The Victory Press*, Donna Spencer, Brian McFarlane, and many more, we would have lost even more history than we already have.

Karissa Donkin writes about women's hockey and the PWHL for CBC Sports and has worked in newspapers and broadcasting for more than a decade. Since 2016, she has been working with CBC's Atlantic investigative unit, covering stories that regularly air on national programs across all of CBC's platforms. Her recent work on New Brunswick's Child Protective Services was profiled on *The Current*. She has won a National Newspaper Award and several Atlantic Journalism Awards for her investigative work. Her journalism was also nominated for the prestigious Michener Award. *Breakaway* is her first book.

Photo: Meaghan Mayo